FINANCIAL WORDS AND TERMS
EVERY CHILD SHOULD KNOW
OVER 100 FUN FLASHCARDS

APPRECIATION

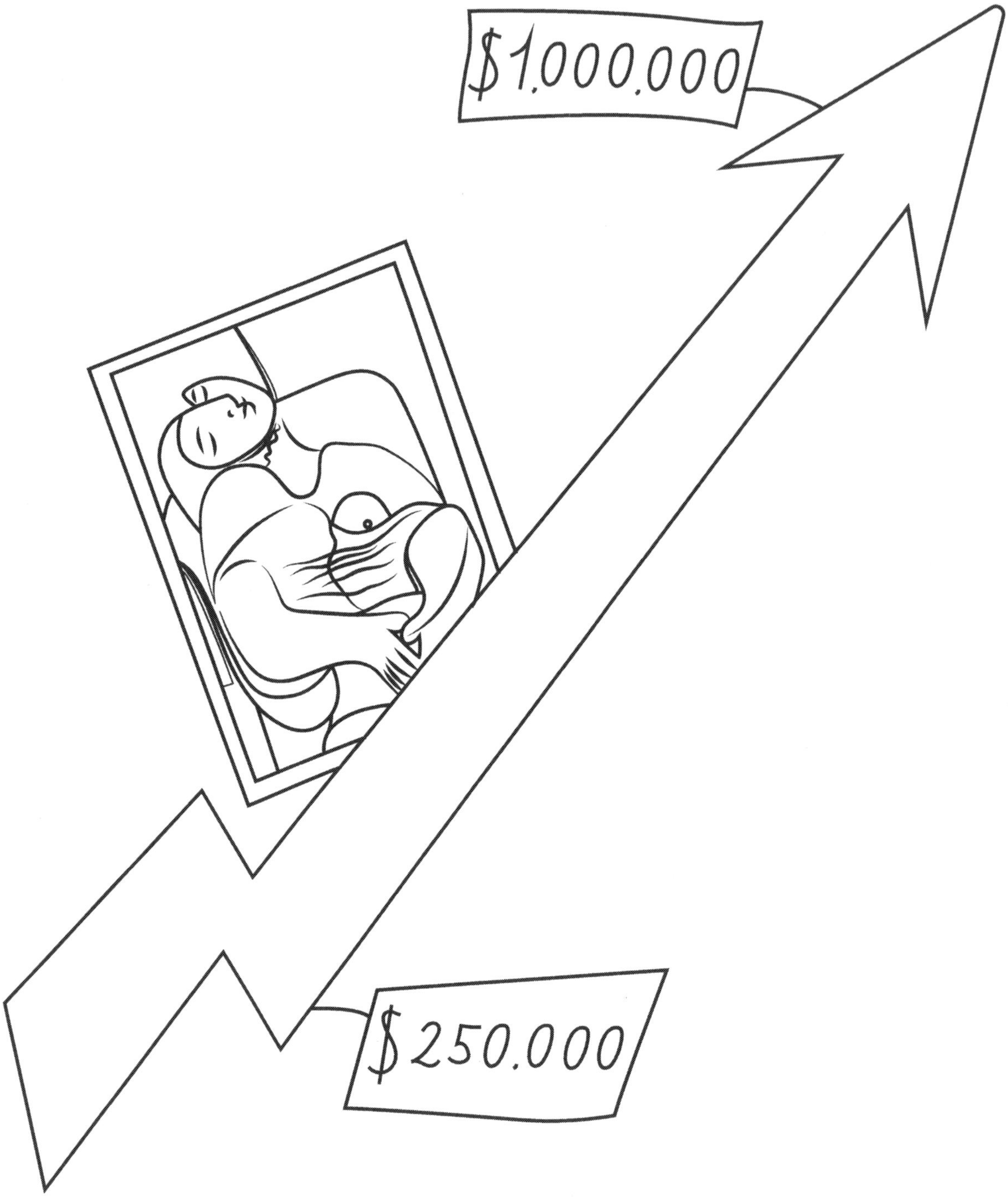

APPRECIATION: When something increases in value.

ASSET

ASSET: An item with economic value that a person or organization owns, such as stocks, real estate, personal property, and business equipment.

BANK

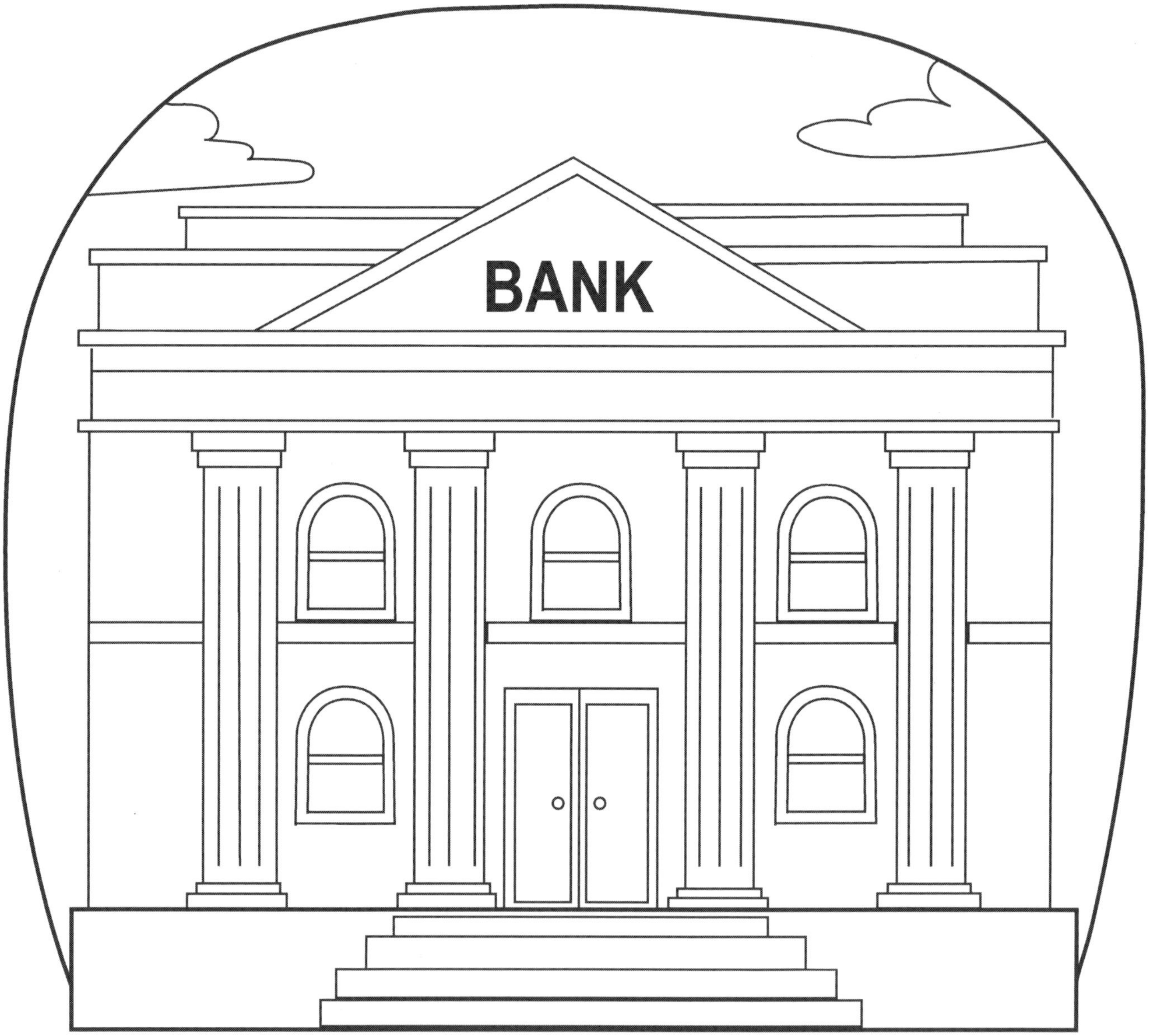

BANK: A financial institution that is licensed to receive deposits, offer loans, and provide other financial services.

BANKRUPT

BANKRUPT: Describes a person or organization who has been declared by law as unable to pay the debts they owe.

BOND

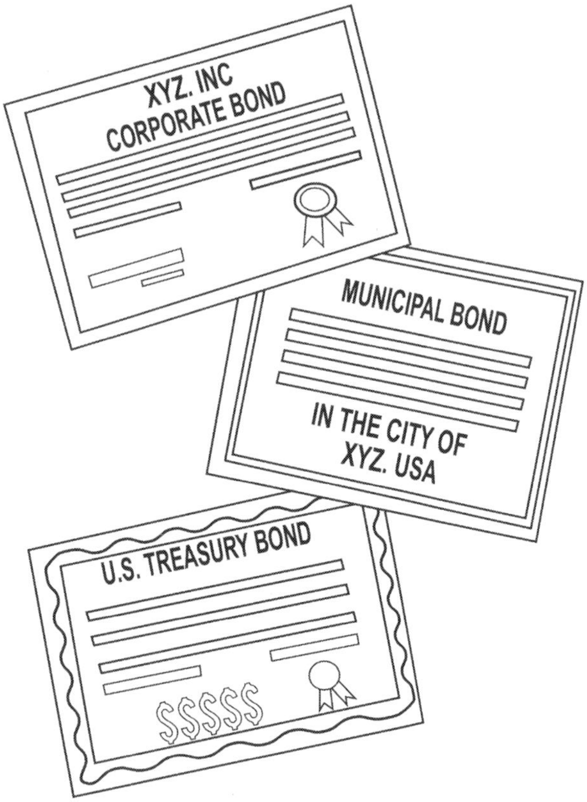

A certificate showing that a buyer agrees to lend a business or government money, on the promise that the borrower will pay back the debt—with interest—at a specific time.

Based on the definition of bond and volatility (see glossary) would you describe a bond as having high or low volatility?

Explain: ____

____

____

____

____

BUDGET

A spending plan or a record of expected and actual income and expenses over a period.

Unscramble the words.

GDTEUB ____________________

NEMOY ____________________

SCTO ____________________

LAPN ____________________

NCIEOM ____________________

GNIEPSND ____________________

Do you think having a budget is important? Why?

____

____

____

Answers: Budget, Money, Cost, Plan, Income, and Spending.

BUSINESS OWNER

BUSINESS OWNER: A person or group that owns and profits from a system (business) and its assets without having to be present.

CAPITAL

Money available to invest.

You just completed a fundraiser, and you now have $250,000 in capital. What will you invest the capital in?

Explain: ____

____

____

____

____

____

CHECKING ACCOUNT

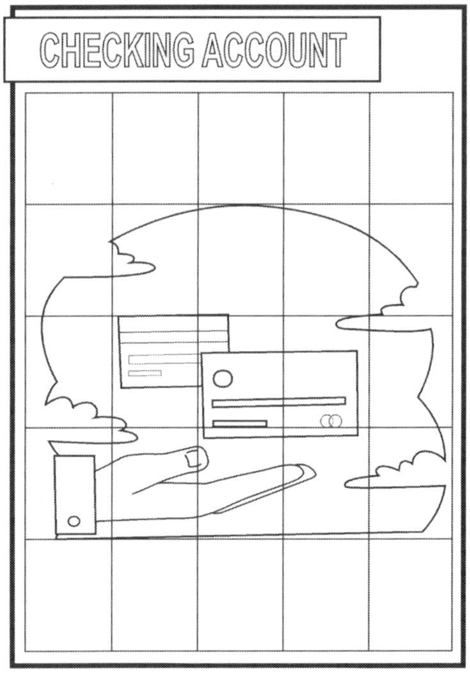

An account that typically holds the money you're using for bill payments and living expenses, usually paying little to no interest.

Use the **grid** to help **draw** the picture!

COLLECTION AGENCY

COLLECTION AGENCY: A business that specializes in obtaining payments from debtors who have defaulted on their loans.

COMPARISON SHOPPING

The process of seeking information about products and services to find the best quality or use at the best price.

You are shopping for a camera with basic functions. You have $150.00 to spend. Which camera would you go with and why?

A) Camera A is a well-known brand. It has everything you want in a camera and much more. The product has a lot of great reviews but it is out of your budget with a cost of $225.00. There is a one year warranty included.

B) Camera B is not a well-known brand. It only has three reviews but they are good. It is priced at $145.00. The description says that they do not offer a warranty.

C) Camera C is a well-known brand and it cost $125.00. There are a lot of reviews and most are average. The product comes with a two year warranty included.

CONTENTMENT

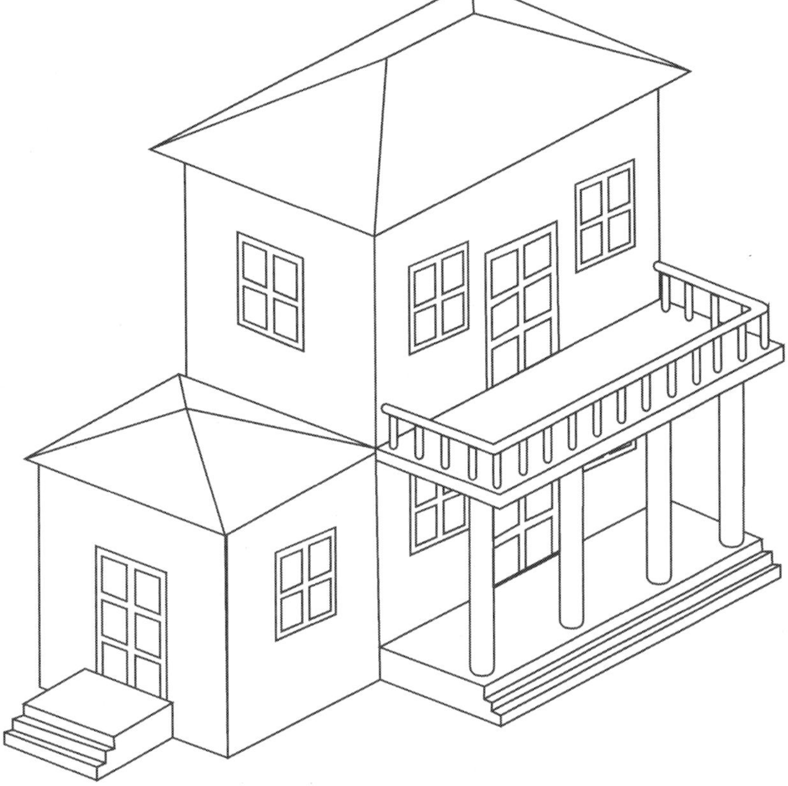

CONTENTMENT: Being happy with what you have.

CREDIT

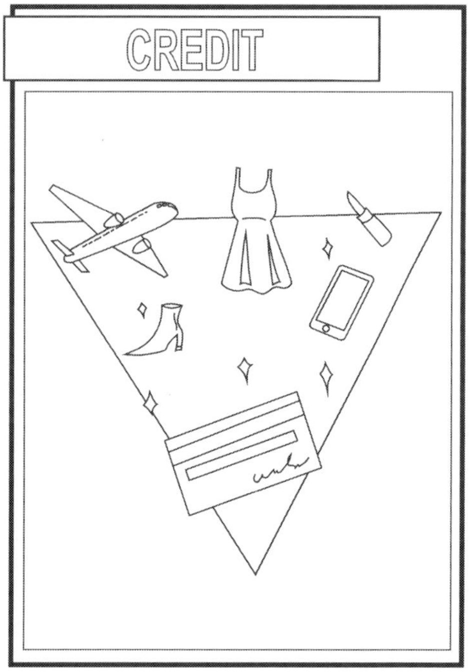

An agreement to provide goods, services, or money in exchange for future payments with interest by a specific date or according to a specific schedule; the use of someone else's money for a fee.

Based on the above definition is credit a form of debt?

Yes or No

Explain: ______________________________________

____

____

____

____

____

DEBT

DEBT: An amount of money owed to a person, bank, company, etc.

DEPRECIATION

DEPRECIATION: When something decreases in value.

EARNED INCOME

EARNED INCOME: Earnings from a job, including commissions and tips.

ECONOMY

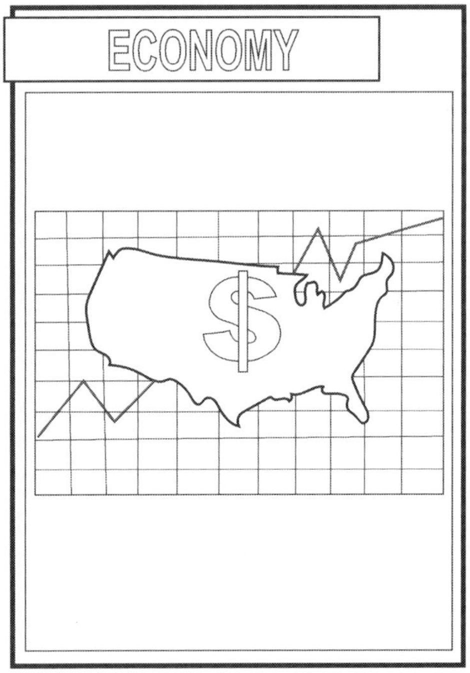

The wealth and resources of a country or region, especially from the goods and services it produces and consumes.

Unscramble the words.

OOEYMNC ________________

TWHAEL ________________

ORPCUDE ________________

OOSDG ________________

EMNOCSU ________________

SERESCIV ________________

Do you think your country's economy is currently strong or weak? Explain your answer.

____

____

____

Answers: Economy, Wealth, Produce, Goods, Consume, and Services.

EMERGENCY FUND

Decode the Secret Message!

1= A
2= B
3= C
4= D
5= E
6= F
7= G
8= H
9= I
10= J
11= K
12= L
13= M

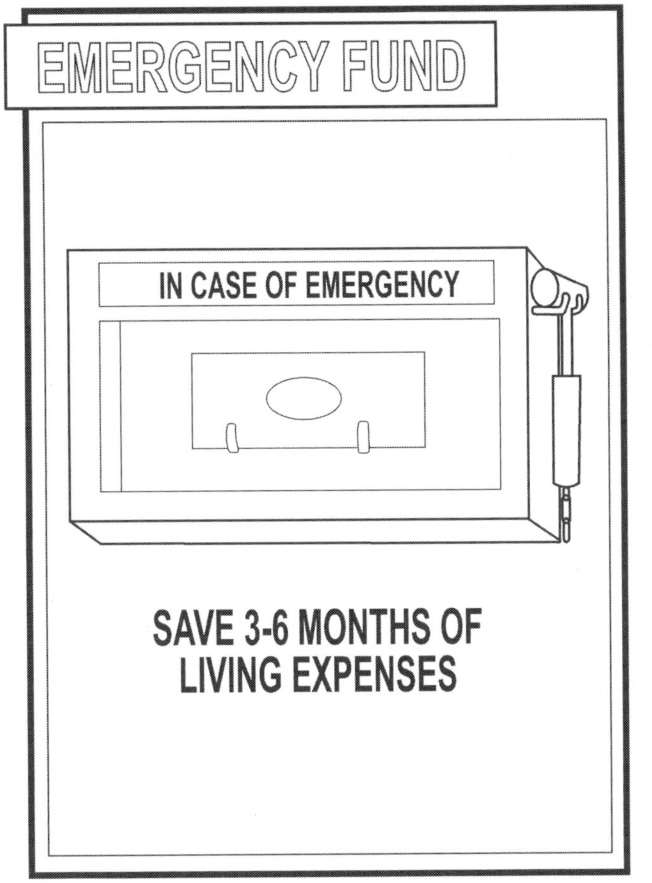

14= N
15= O
16= P
17= Q
18= R
19= S
20= T
21= U
22= V
23= W
24= X
25= Y
26= Z

13 15 14 5 25   19 5 20   1 19 9 4 5   6 15 18

21 14 5 24 16 5 3 20 5 4   5 24 16 5 14 19 5 19

15 18   6 15 18   12 9 22 9 14 7   3 15 19 20 19

9 14   3 1 19 5   15 6   10 15 2   12 15 19 19

Answer: Money set aside for unexpected expenses or for living costs in case of job loss.

EMPLOYEE

EMPLOYEE: Someone who works for someone else in exchange for wages or a salary.

EXPENSE

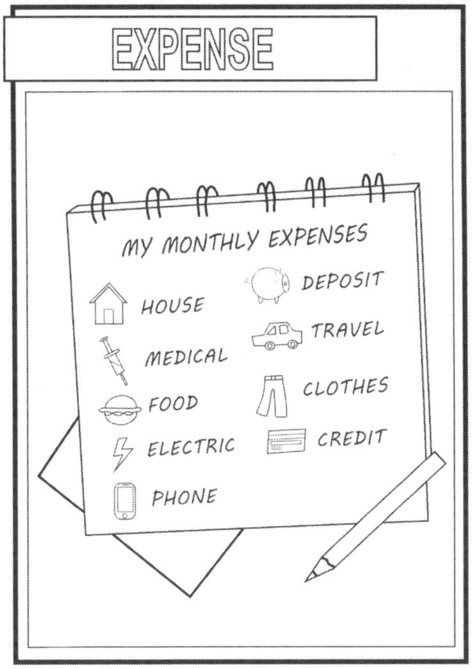

The cost required for something; the money spent on something.

Jacob has a lawn mowing company that he runs after school and on the weekends. Circle the expenses that Jacob is likely to have operating his lawn mowing company.

Gas	Candy	Paper	Parts	Tools
Wood	Shirts	Crayons	Cooler	Gum
Flyers	Toys	Tool Box	Balloons	Oil

Answer: Gas, Flyers, Tool Box, Parts, Tools, Oil.

FINANCIAL ADVISER

FINANCIAL ADVISER: A person who provides financial information and advice.

GOODS

Items that are usually (but not always tangible, such as pens, salt, apples, and hats.

If you could make your own product (Good) what would it be? How would it be different from similar products?

IMPULSE BUYING

IMPULSE BUYING: The buying of goods or services without planning ahead, as a result of a sudden whim or impulse; the buyer often does not consider their needs, goals, or consequences.

INCOME

INCOME: Money received, especially on a regular basis, for work or through investments.

INVESTMENT

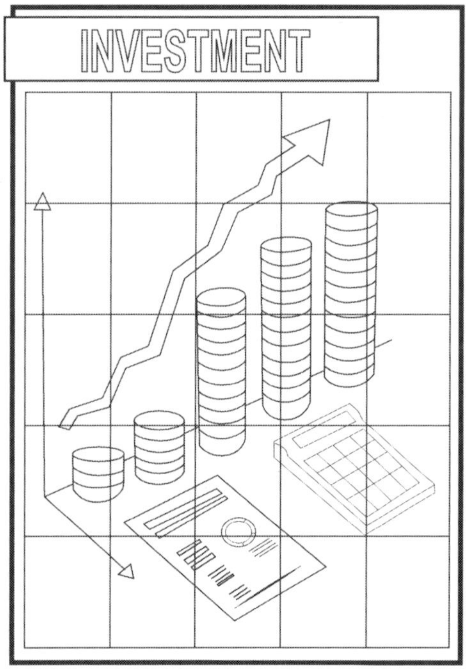

The action or process of contributing money to earn a profit or material result.

Use the **grid** to help **draw** the picture!

INVESTOR

INVESTOR: A person or organization that puts money into financial plans, property, etc., expecting to earn a profit.

LIABILITY

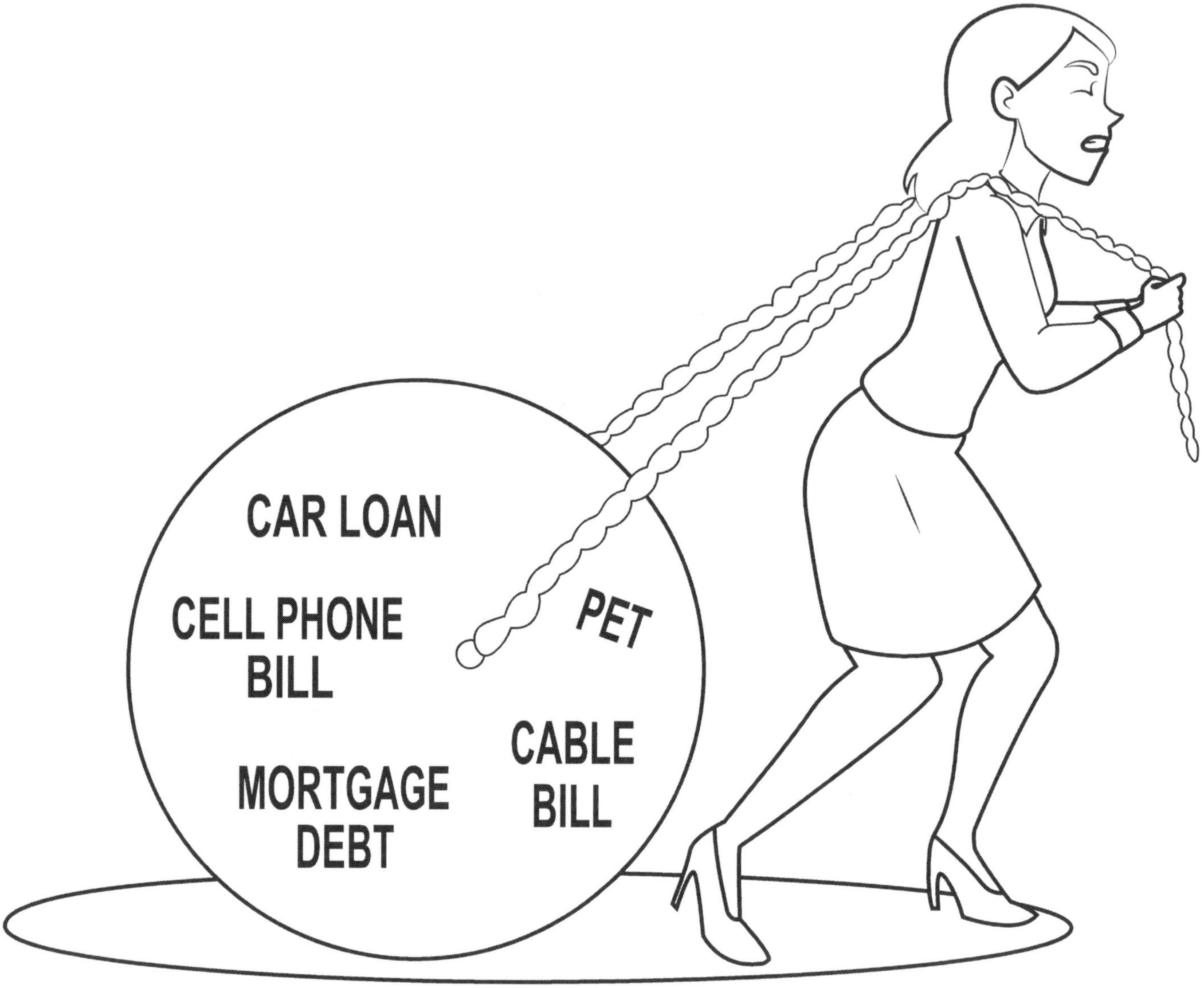

LIABILITY: A debt or financial obligation.

LOAN

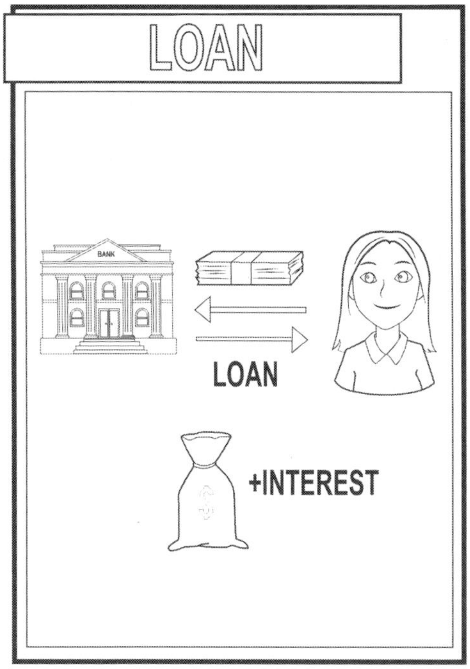

A thing that is borrowed, especially an amount of money that is expected to be paid back with interest.

Most people take out a loan to purchase a vehicle. The average new car payment is $509 a month. People who are financially smart pay cash for slightly used vehicles. If you were to invest $509 monthly you could be a millionaire within 30 years.

You may ask how that is possible. $509 x 12 = $6,108 and $6,108 x 30 = $183,240.

$183,240 is clearly not $1,000,000.

What you are seeing here is the power of investing and compounding.

Would you rather buy a new car or a used car? Why? Also, would you rather take a loan out for a car or pay for it in full? Why?

LOSS

An amount of money lost by a business or organization.

Having a rental property comes with quite a few expenses. Below is your income statement for your property in the next state over.

Total income for the year: $12,000
Expenses: Repairs $3,000, Management Fee $1,800, Insurance $950, Property Taxes $1,250, Depreciation $3,400, Lawn Service $1,600, and Traveling Cost $2,000.

Use the below space to calculate the loss.

Answer: Loss of $2,000.

NEEDS

Things you need to survive.

Julie is having a hard time separating her needs from her wants. Help Julie identify her needs by circling them below.

Food	Shelter	Mansion	New Car	Clothes
Newest Phone	Designer Clothes	Candy	Medicine	Vacation
Electricity	Water	Gardner	Pet	Jewelry

Answer: Food, Shelter, Clothes, Medicine, Electricity, and Water

PAY YOURSELF FIRST

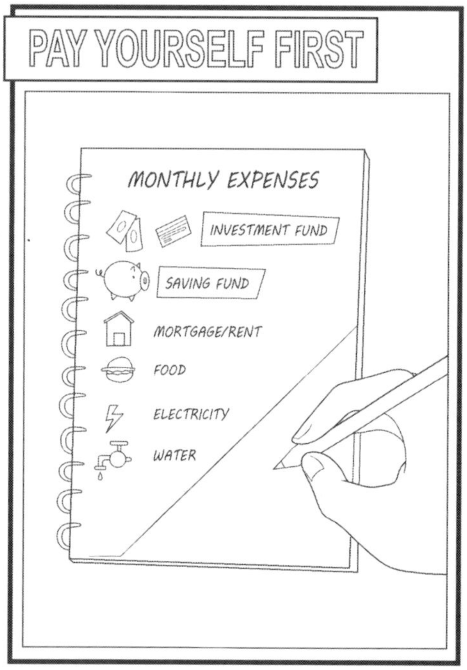

The practice of setting aside a portion of all the money you receive for saving and investing before paying other expenses.

How many words can you think of using the letters below?

PAY YOURSELF FIRST

PROFIT

PROFIT

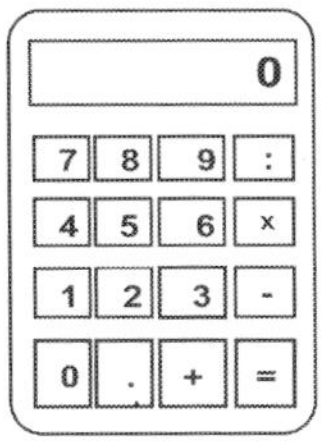

PROFIT FORMULA

PROFIT=

TOTAL SALES- TOTAL EXPENSES

The money earned after subtracting total costs from the total revenue of a business or investment.

Can you calculate the profit for each of the below business ventures?

Cole has a vending machine business that he operates after school and on the weekends. His total sales for the month is $789. He has the following expenses: Inventory = $250, Rent= $78, and Gas= $25.

What is Cole's total expenses?

What is Cole's profit?

Earned Income/ Unearned Income

Cole bought a carpet cleaning machine for $150. His only other expense was the cleaning solution in which he bought in bulk for $50. He charges $25 for large rooms and $15 for small rooms. In one month he has cleaned ten small rooms and twenty large rooms.

What is Cole's total expenses?
What is Cole's total sales?
What is Cole's profit?

Earned Income/ Unearned Income

Answer: $353, $436, Earned Income, $200, $650, $450, Earned Income.

RENT

RENT: A regular fee for the use of property.

REVENUE

Income received from the sale of a product or service.

Help Tiffany calculate her total revenue for the weekend from her laundromat business.

Her earnings for the weekend were:
Sat: $275, and Sun: $335

Calculate the total revenue.

Answer Key: $610.

RISK

RISK: A measure of chance a loss will happen or an investment will bring a good rate of return.

SAVINGS ACCOUNT

SAVINGS ACCOUNT: A deposit account at a bank or other financial institution that earns interest; it typically pays a modest interest rate, but is safe and reliable, a great way to store cash for short-term needs.

SELF-EMPLOYED

SELF-EMPLOYED: Describes someone who works for themselves rather than working for an employer.

SERVICE

SERVICE: Work done by other people, such as doctors, lawn care workers, dentists, barbers, and waiters.

TICKER SYMBOL

TICKER SYMBOL

JOHNSON AND JOHNSON (NYSE: JNJ)

CISCO (NYSE: CSCO)

CATERPILLAR (NYSE: CAT)

MCDONALDS (NYSE: MCD)

UNITED TECHNOLOGIES (NYSE: UTX)

A set of characters—usually letters— representing securities listed on an exchange or otherwise traded publicly.

Can you fill in the information for the below companies? Hint: Research "Company + Stock".

Company Name	Ticker Symbol	52 Week High	52 Week Low	Does the company pay a dividend? Y or N
NIKE				
WAL-MART				
DISNEY				

WANTS

WANTS: Things you do not need to survive.

WEALTH

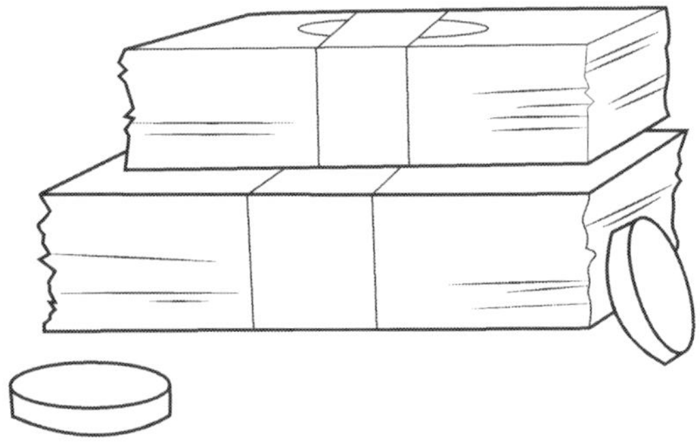

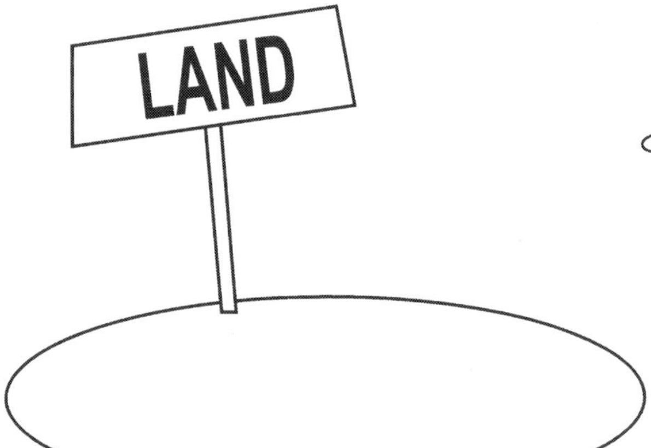

WEALTH: The value of all the assets of worth owned by a person, community, company, or country.

401(k)

401(k): A company-sponsored retirement account that employees can use to save money. Employers may also contribute the same amount.

52 WEEK HIGH

Solve the Maze!

52 WEEK HIGH

STATS

OPEN	30.17
HIGH	30.25
LOW	29.93
52 WK HIGH	35.67
52 WK LOW	17.95
VOLUME	33.28M
AVG VOL	53.36M
MKT CAP	259.61B
P/E RATIO	14.81
DIV/YIELD	2.40

The highest price at which a security, such as a stock, has traded during a time period equal to one year.

What is the ticker symbol of your favorite stock?

What is the 52 Week High of your favorite stock?

52 WEEK LOW

Solve the Maze!

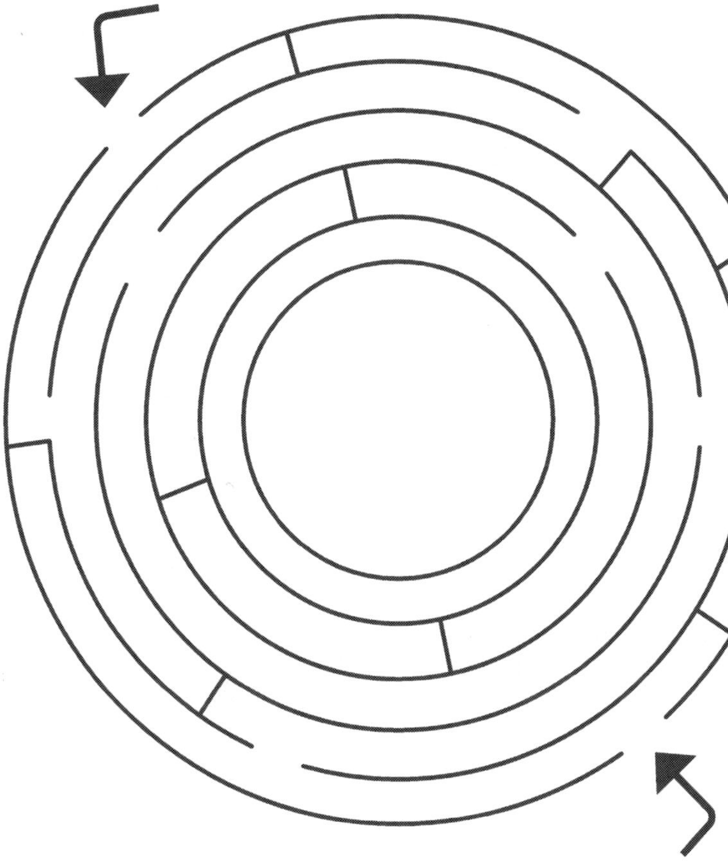

52 WEEK LOW

STATS

OPEN	30.17
HIGH	30.25
LOW	29.93
52 WK HIGH	35.67
52 WK LOW	17.95
VOLUME	33.28M
AVG VOL	53.36M
MKT CAP	259.61B
P/E RATIO	14.81
DIV/YIELD	2.40

The lowest price at which a security, such as a stock, has traded during a time period equal to one year.

What is the ticker symbol of your favorite stock?

What is the 52 Week Low of your favorite stock?

ANNUAL REPORT

A corporate document issued to shareholders that spells out the company's financial condition and operations over the previous year.

Find and **Circle** the words below...

ANNUAL
REPORT
COMPANY
FINANCIAL
DOCUMENT
PREVIOUS
YEAR

F	I	N	A	N	C	I	A	L	M
D	O	C	U	M	E	N	T	V	D
P	R	E	V	I	O	U	S	L	Z
L	B	W	C	O	M	P	A	N	Y
A	N	N	U	A	L	Y	E	A	R
R	E	P	O	R	T	T	W	B	B
Y	Z	J	Y	R	D	J	D	G	R
R	D	W	N	D	V	B	Y	G	Z

ANNUITY

ANNUITY: A fixed amount of money paid to someone each year, typically for the rest of their life.

BENEFICIARY

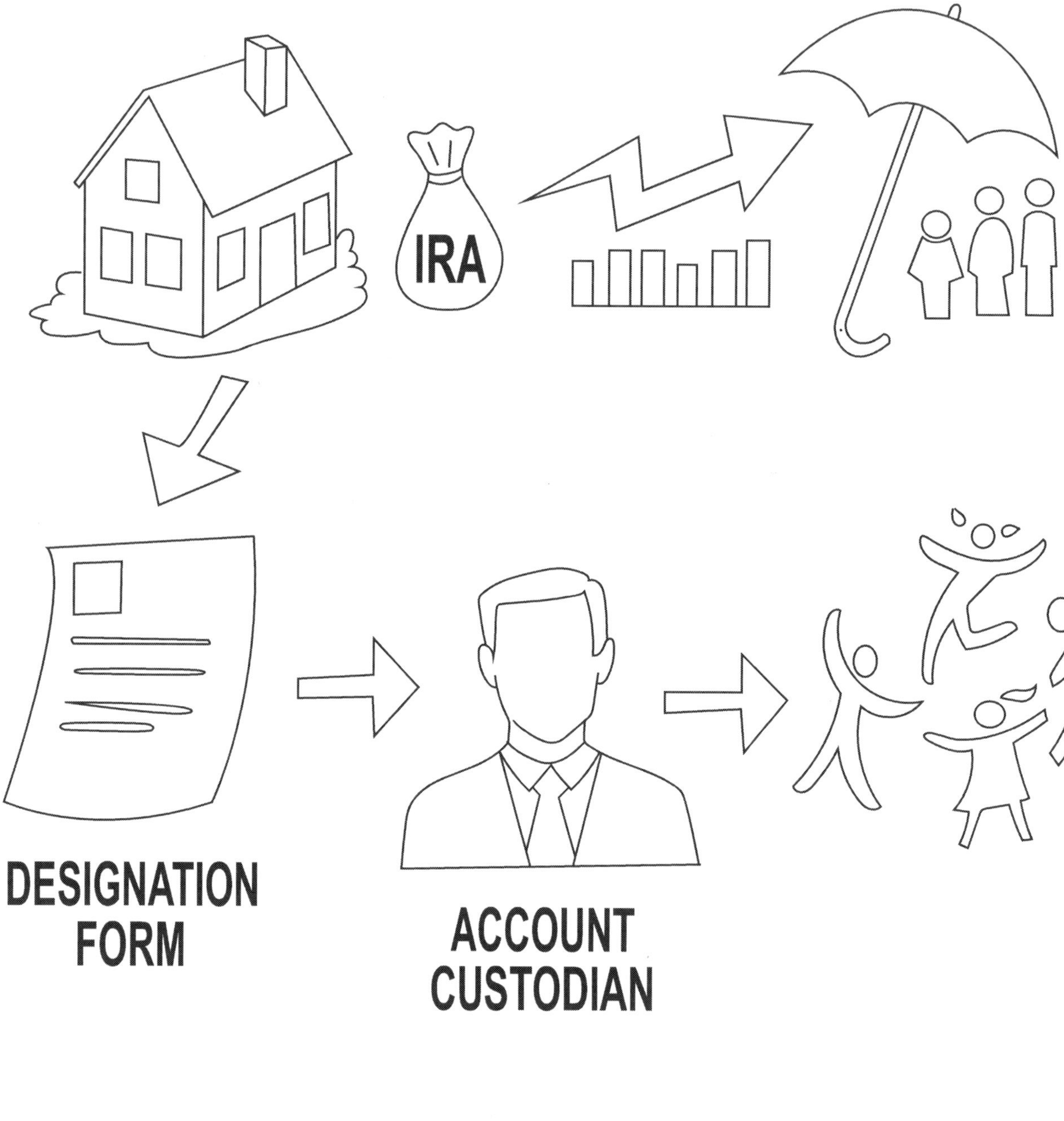

BENEFICIARY: A person or organization named to receive assets after someone dies.

BROKERAGE ACCOUNT

An account to keep cash, liquid money, in for investing in stocks, bonds, mutual funds, and other investments.

How many words can you think of using the letters below?

BROKERAGE ACCOUNT

CAPITAL GAIN

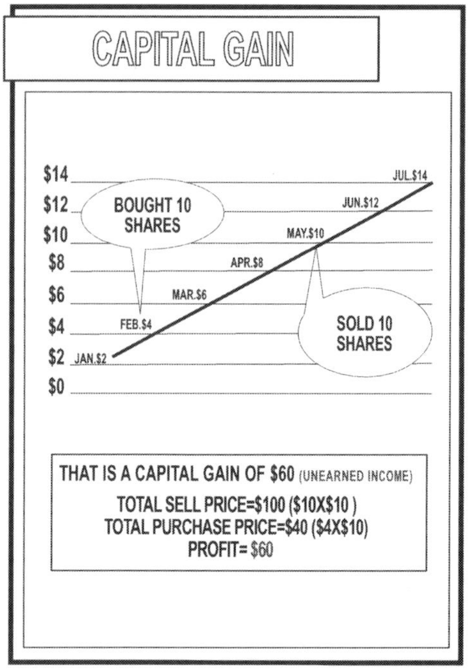

Income from selling an asset for more than the original purchase price.

What is the capital gain for the following investment?

At the beginning of the year Ashley bought ten shares of her favorite stock for $10 per share. At the end of the year she sold all her stock for the new price of $25.

How much was Ashley's principal investment? _______X_______ = _______

How much was Ashley's total sell price? _______X_______ = _______

What is Ashley's capital gain from this investment? _______ - _______ = _______

Answer: $100, $250, and $150.

CAPITAL LOSS

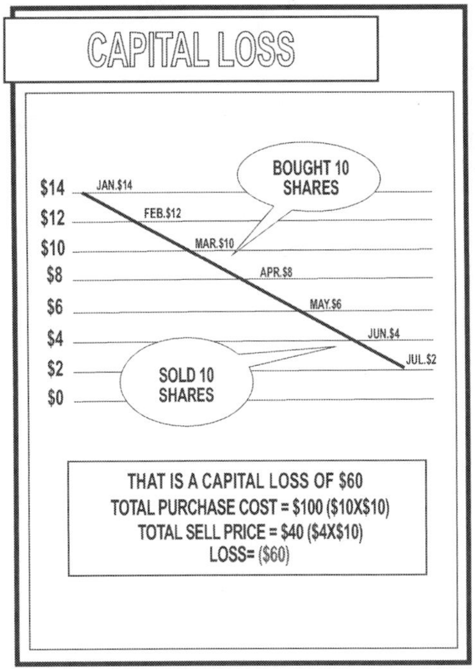

A financial loss from selling an asset for less than the original purchase price.

What is the capital loss for the following investment?

At the beginning of the year Jayce bought twenty shares of her favorite stock for $5 per share. At the end of the year she sold all her stock for the new price of $2 per share.

How much was Jayce's principal investment? ______ X ______ = ______

How much was Jayce's total sell price? ______ X ______ = ______

What is Jayce's capital loss from this investment? ______ - ______ = ______

Answer: $100, $40, $60.

COLLATERAL

COLLATERAL: Property that a borrower promises to give up to a lender in case of default.

CONTRACT

A legally binding agreement between two or more parties.

Circle The Picture That is Different.

CREDIT REPORT

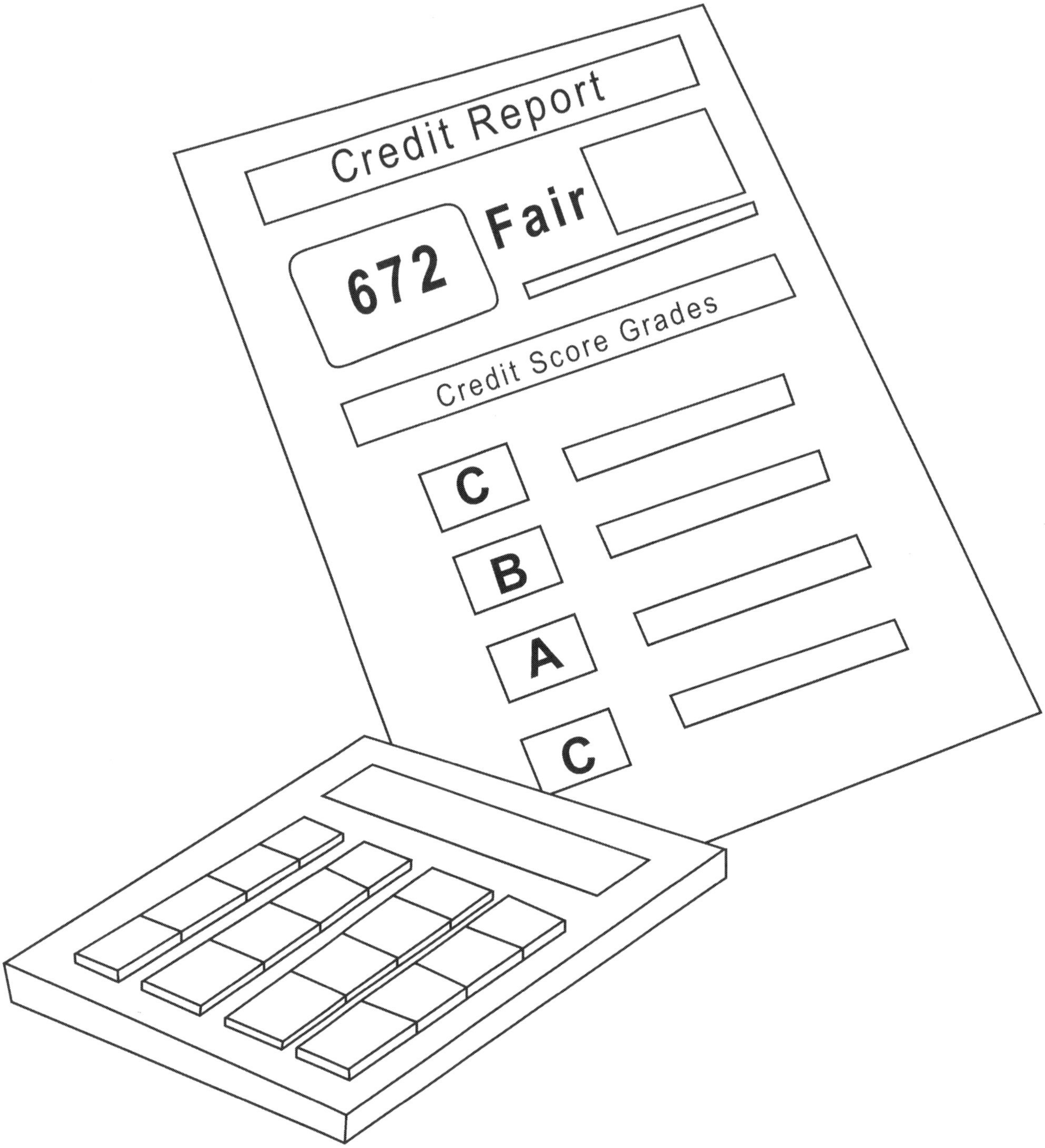

CREDIT REPORT: An official record of a borrower's credit history, including such information as the amount and type of credit used, outstanding balances, and any delinquencies, bankruptcies, or tax liens.

CREDIT SCORE

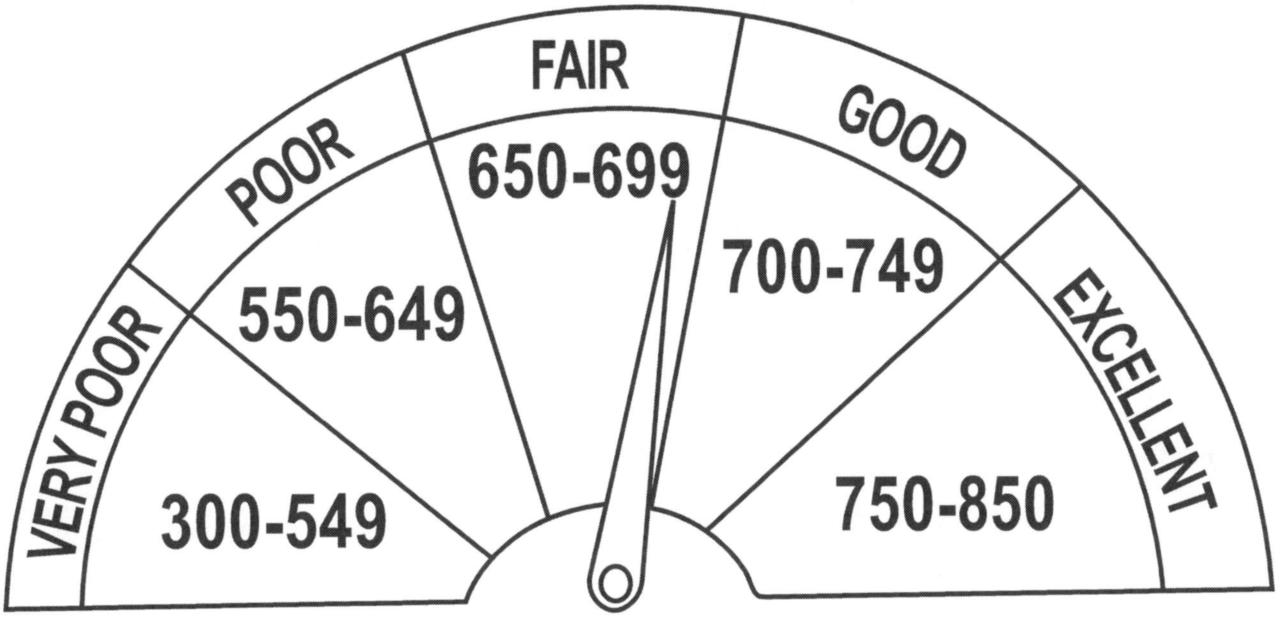

CREDIT SCORE: A measure of how likely a person applying for a loan is to pay the debt back, based on previous debt repayment.

DAY HIGH

Solve the Maze!

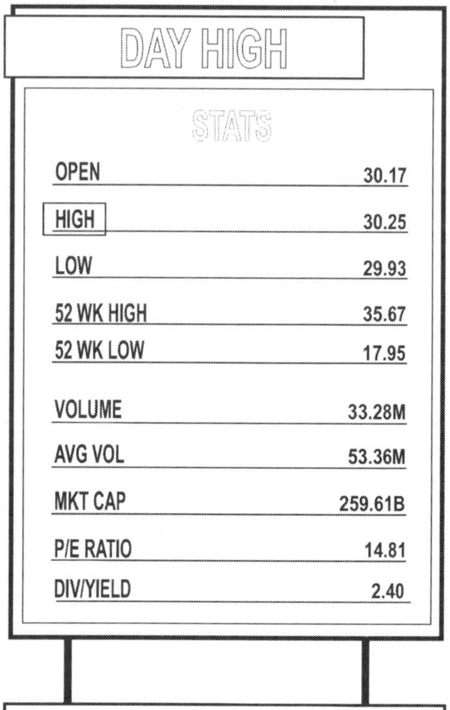

The highest price at which a security, such as a stock, has traded that day.

What is the ticker symbol of your favorite stock?

What is the Day High of your favorite stock?

DAY LOW

Solve the Maze!

DAY LOW

STATS

OPEN	30.17
HIGH	30.25
LOW	29.93
52 WK HIGH	35.67
52 WK LOW	17.95
VOLUME	33.28M
AVG VOL	53.36M
MKT CAP	259.61B
P/E RATIO	14.81
DIV/YIELD	2.40

The lowest price at which a security, such as a stock, has traded that day.

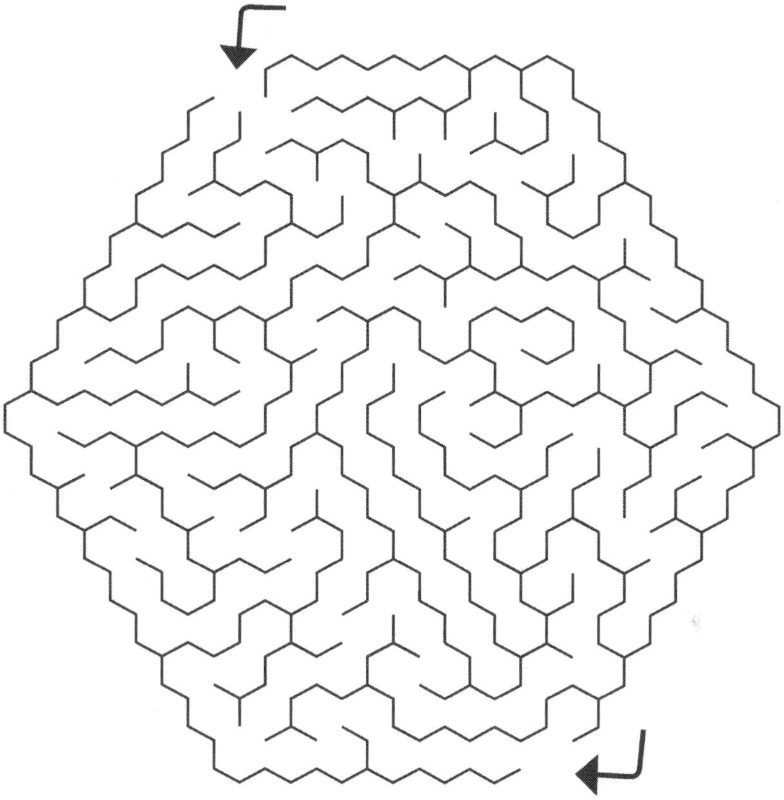

What is the ticker symbol of your favorite stock?

What is the Day Low of your favorite stock?

DEFAULT

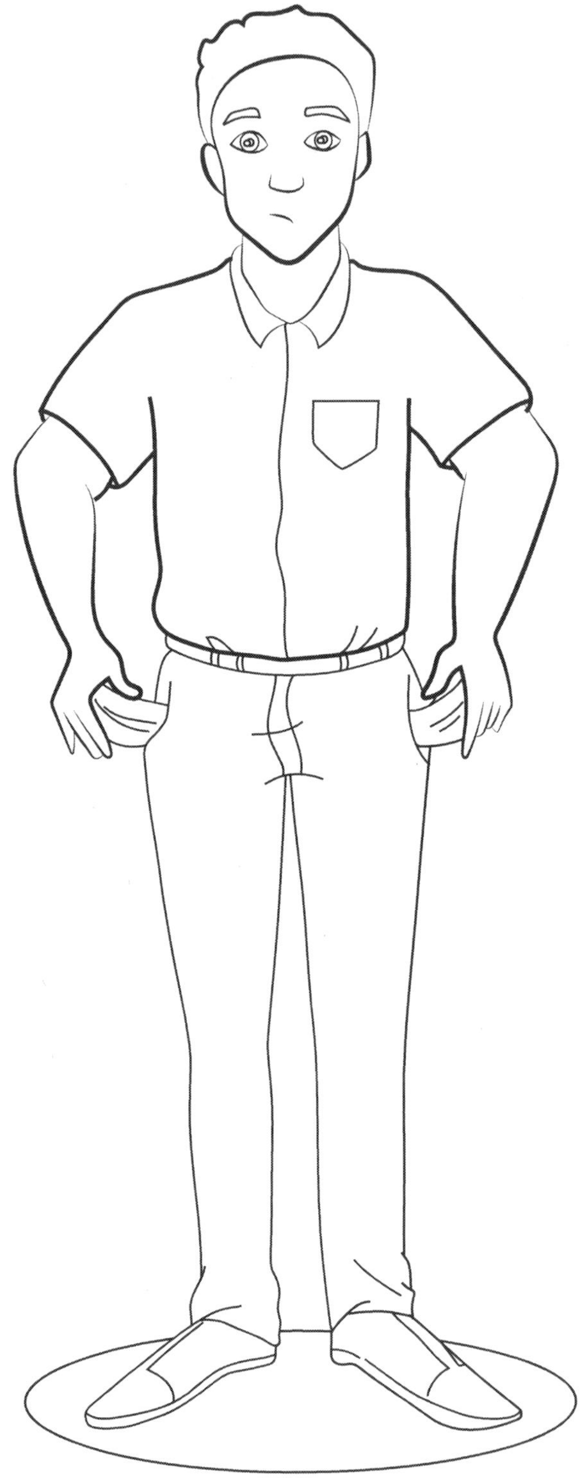

DEFAULT: Failure to pay a debt or keep a financial agreement.

DISPOSABLE INCOME

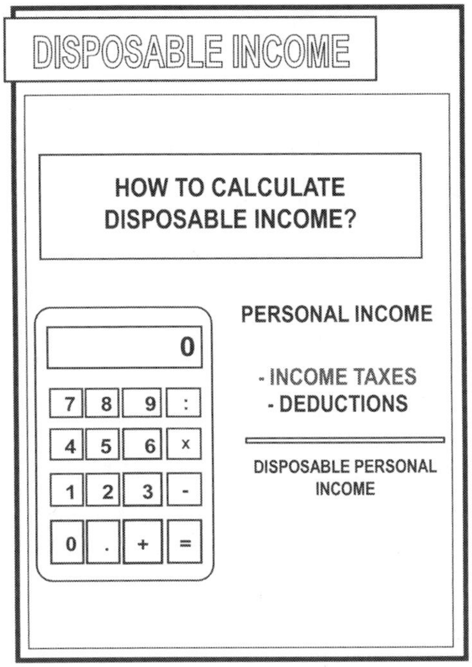

The amount of money a household has available for spending and saving after paying income taxes.

Using the above picture as a guide, what is the disposable income?

Income:

$500.00

Deductions:

$50 – 401(k)

$110- Federal Taxes

$40- Medical

Answer: $300.

DIVIDENDS

DIVIDENDS: Payments made by publicly listed companies to reward investors for putting their money into the venture.

ESTATE

ESTATE: All the money and property owned by a particular person, especially at death.

FINANCE CHARGE

FINANCE CHARGE: A fee charged for the use of credit, which may be a flat fee or a percentage of the amount borrowed; for example, a $100 loan repaid with $9 interest plus a $1 service fee has a finance charge of $10.

FINANCIAL PLAN

FINANCIAL PLAN: A document containing a person's current money situation and long-term monetary goals, as well as ways to achieve those goals.

FORECLOSURE

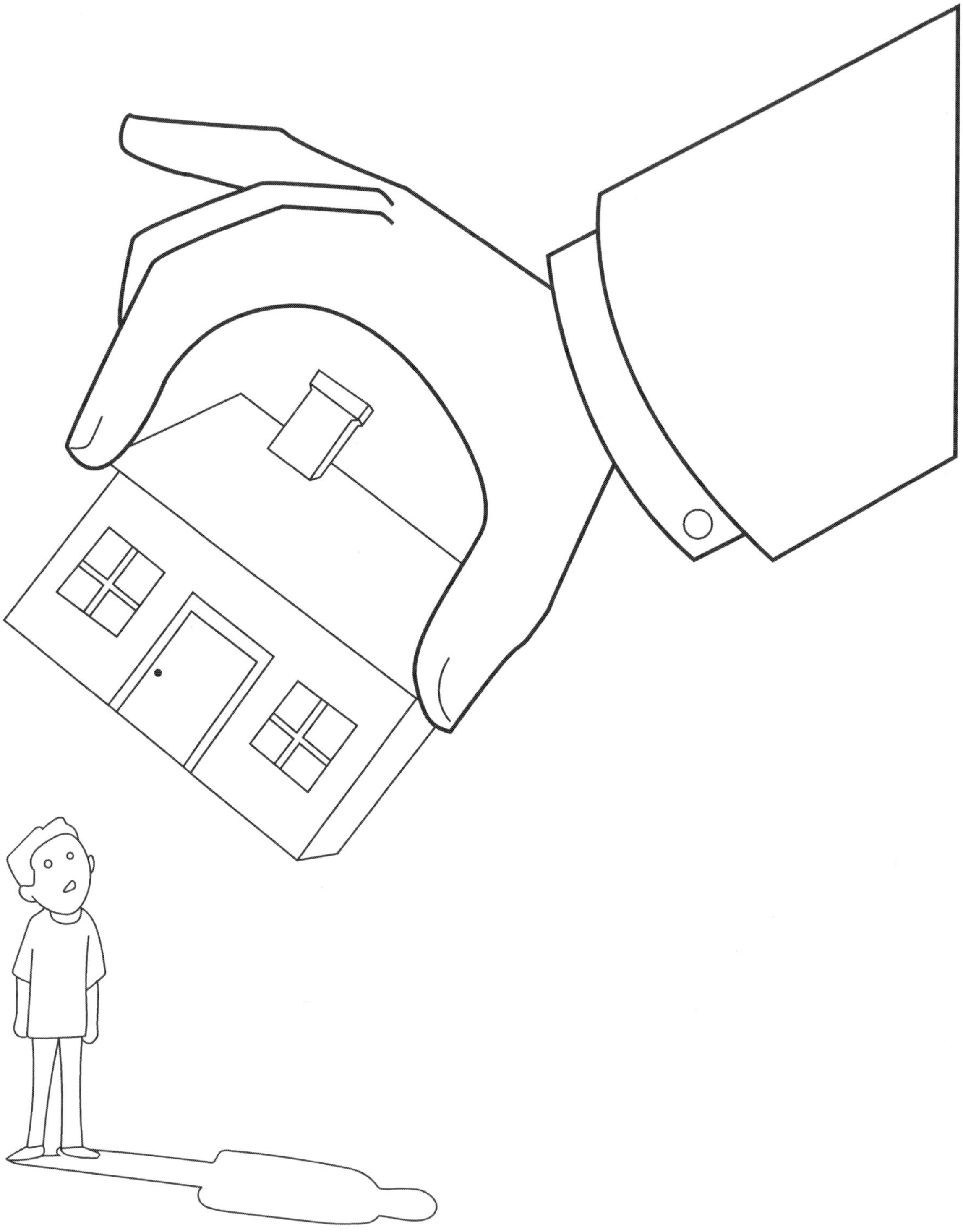

FORECLOSURE: A process in which homeowners lose their property because they have failed to make mortgage payments and it becomes the property of the bank.

FORTUNE 500

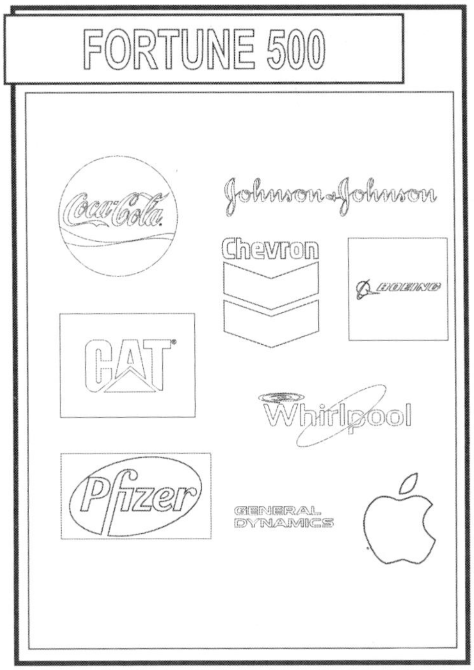

An annual list of the 500 most profitable US industrial corporations.

Choose from these companies and record their information below.

Company Name	Ticker Symbol	52 Week High	52 Week Low	Does the company pay a dividend? Y or N

GARNISHMENT

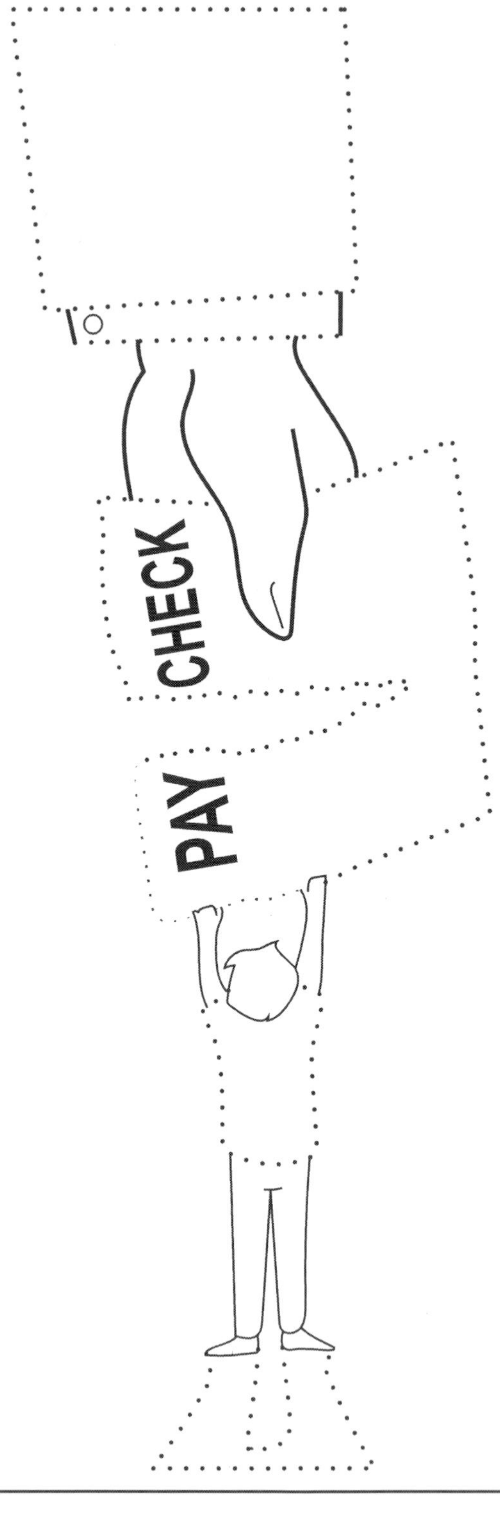

CONNECT the DOTS

GARNISHMENT: When a court sets aside part of an employee's wages to pay a debt.

GRACE PERIOD

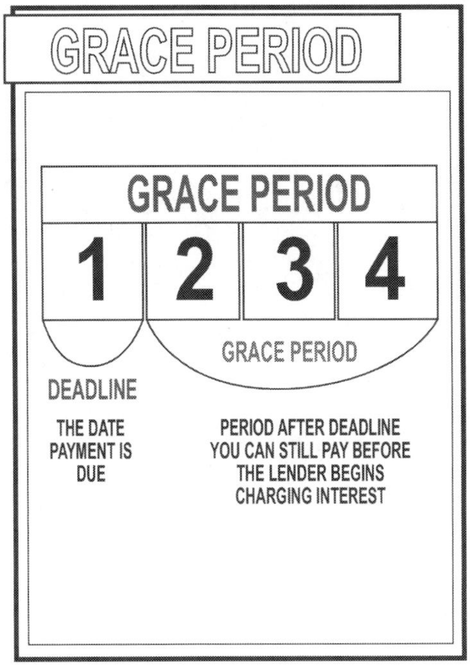

A time given for a borrower to pay the full balance of credit due and not incur finance charges or pay an insurance premium without penalty.

How many words can you think of using the letters below?

GRACE PERIOD

GROSS PAY

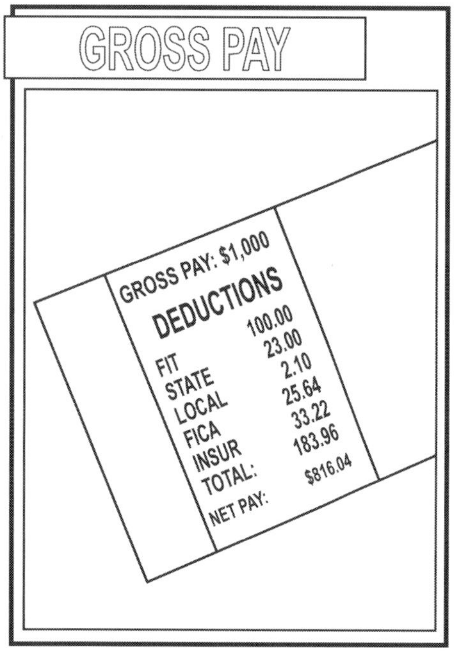

The amount of salary or wages earned by an employee before any deductions or contributions are subtracted, such as taxes.

Find and **Circle** the words below...

- GROSS
- TAXES
- PAY
- EMPLOYEE
- SALARY
- DEDUCTIONS
- WAGES
- INSURANCE

D	E	D	U	C	T	I	O	N	S
E	C	N	A	R	U	S	N	I	G
M	S	N	J	T	E	G	Y	B	P
P	A	M	N	X	R	J	Z	Q	Q
L	L	N	A	O	W	A	G	E	S
O	A	T	S	P	T	K	K	J	Y
Y	R	S	B	M	A	Y	Y	Z	K
E	Y	M	Y	Y	T	Y	R	N	T
E	R	Q	Z	M	J	B	L	V	X

INHERITANCE

INHERITANCE: Money or property that is passed from one person to another upon the owner's death.

INSURANCE

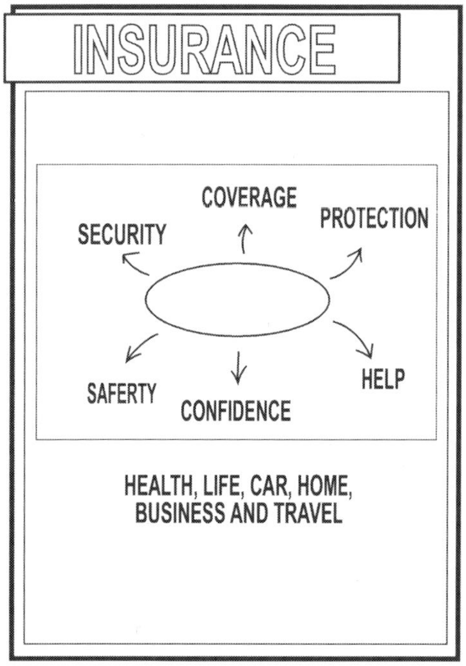

A risk management tool that protects a person from specific financial losses under specific terms and premium payments, as described in a written policy document.

Use these words in the bottom of the image to fill in the blanks.

_______ insurance is generally used when you take trips. It helps pay for things such as lost luggage and cancelations.

_______ insurance decreases the cost for your medical needs.

_______ insurance protects your company.

_______ insurance will help pay to repair your home from damage associated with things like floods, fire, and weather.

_______ insurance will help pay to repair or replace your vehicle in case of damage or theft.

_______ insurance will provide your loved ones with financial stability upon your death.

Key: Travel, Health, Business, Home, Car and Life.

INTERESTQ

INTEREST: The cost of borrowing money and/or the earnings from lending money, which works against you with debt, and for you with investing.

INTEREST INCOME

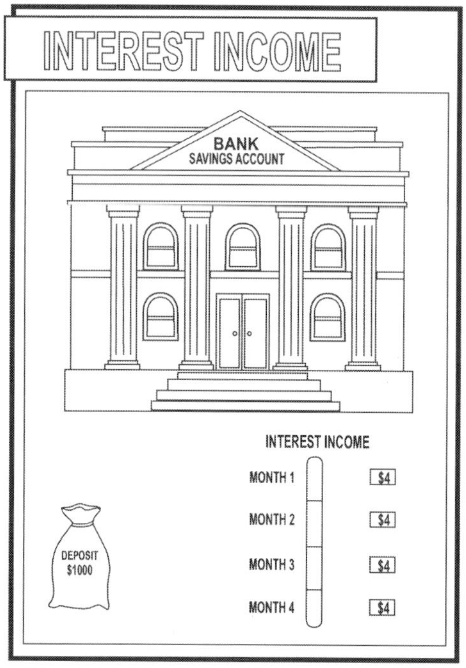

The earnings from lending money.

Match the correct principal (original loan amount) with the correct interest income based on the interest rate. Tip: Use a calculator and covert the interest to a decimal and multiply that by the principal. Example 2% = .02 and 20%=.20.

- $1,000 loan with 2% interest.
- $12,000 loan with 10% interest.
- $30,000 loan with 2% interest.
- $5,000 loan with 10% interest.
- $10,000 loan with 3% interest.
- $1,000 loan with 7% interest.
- $18,000 loan with 4% interest.
- $1,000 loan with 5% interest.

Generates

$600
$500
$50
$20
$70
$720
$1,200
$300

INTEREST RATE

INTEREST RATE: The amount of a loan that the borrower must pay as interest, typically expressed as an annual percentage.

LEASE

LEASE: A contract by which one party lets another use land, property, services, etc. for a specific time, usually in return for a regular payment.

LEVERAGE

LEVERAGE: An investment strategy of using debt to try to make more money on an investment.

MORTGAGE

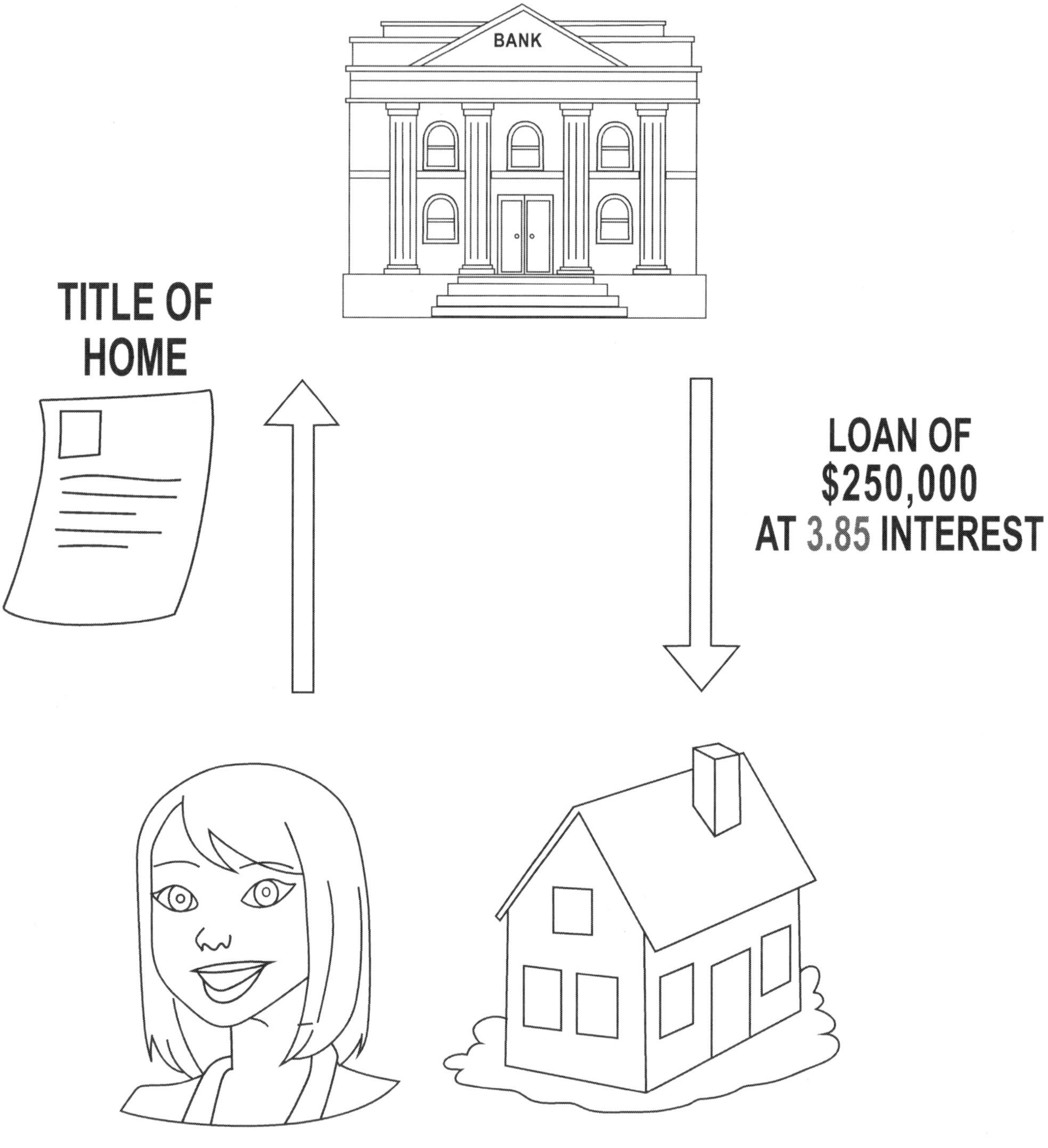

MORTGAGE: A legal agreement by which a bank or other creditor lends money at interest; the lender will own the debtor's property if the debtor defaults on the loan, but not if the debt is paid.

MUTUAL FUND

MUTUAL FUND: A type of investment vehicle made up of a portfolio of stocks, bonds, or other securities.

NET WORTH

NET WORTH= GRAND TOTAL OF ASSETS-LIABILITIES

ASSETS	LIABILITIES
- VALUE OF YOUR HOME - VALUE OF VEHICLES - CHECKING AND SAVINGS ACCOUNTS - CASH - CDs - RETIREMENT ACCOUNTS	- BALANCE ON MORTGAGE OR CAR LOANS - CREDIT CARD DEBT - STUDENT LOAN BALANCE - ANY OTHER DEBT YOU MAY OWE

NET WORTH: A measure of a person's financial condition at a given time, equal to what that person owns (assets) minus what that person owes (liabilities).

PORTFOLIO

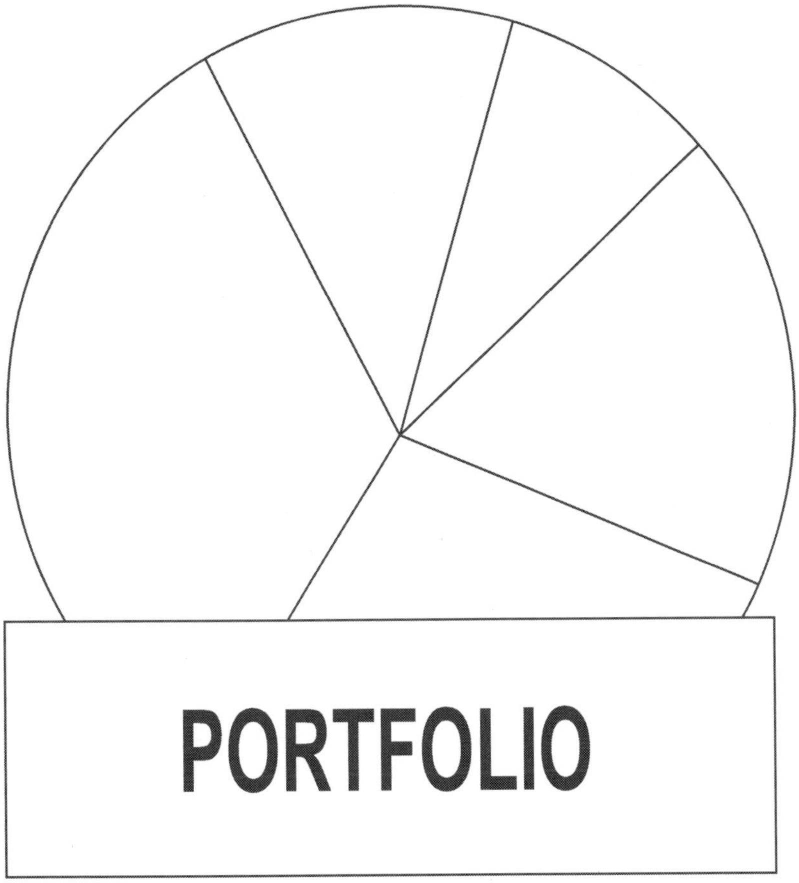

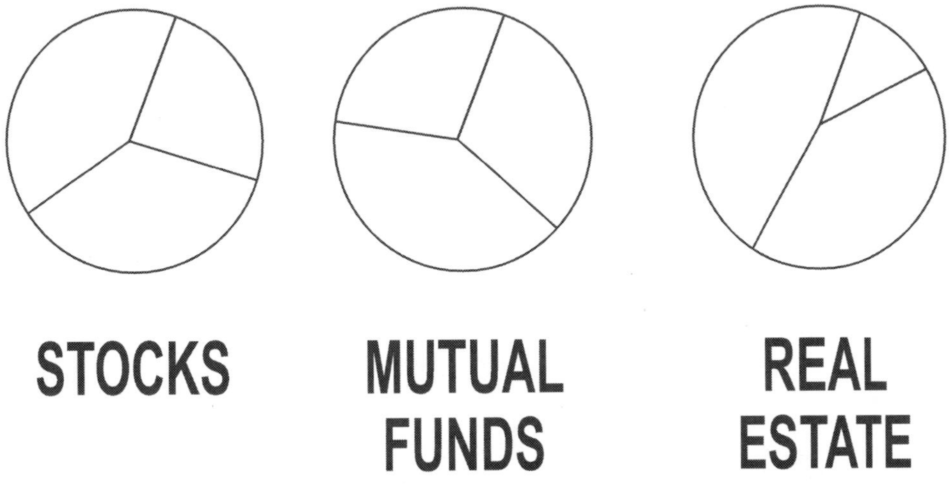

PORTFOLIO: A collection of securities—such as stocks, bonds, mutual funds, and real estate—that an investor owns.

RISK MANAGEMENT

RISK MANAGEMENT: The process of calculating risk and finding ways to lower or manage loss, for example, by buying insurance or diversifying investments.

STOCK

STOCK: An investment that lets the investor own a part of a corporation's assets and earnings.

STOCK MARKET

STOCK MARKET

NEW YORK STOCK EXCHANGE

NASDAQ

LONDON STOCK EXCHANGE

TOKYO STOCK EXCHANGE

EURONEXT

The collection of markets and exchanges where regular buying, selling, and issuance of stock shares of publicly held companies take place.

Research the NASDAQ market and New York Stock Exchange and record three things about each market.

NASDAQ	New York Stock Exchange

TAX

TAX: A government fee on business and personal income, activities, or products.

UNEARNED INCOME

INTEREST INCOME

RENTAL INCOME

DIVIDENDS

UNEARNED INCOME: Earnings from sources other than a job, including investment returns and royalties.

WILL

A legal statement of a person's wishes for giving away his or her estate after death.

Based on the definition of will and estate (see glossary) what are some things you might find in someone's will?

Explain:

BEAR MARKET

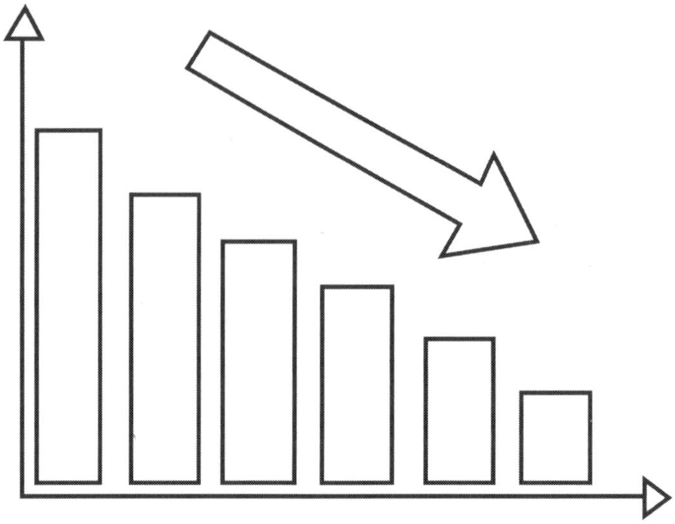

ENCOURAGES SELLING

BEAR MARKET: A time when a market's prices fall for an extended time, usually by 20% or more from recent highs, with negative feelings and low expectations from investors.

BULL MARKET

ENCOURAGES BUYING

BULL MARKET: A time when a financial market's prices are rising or are expected to rise.

COMPOUND INTEREST

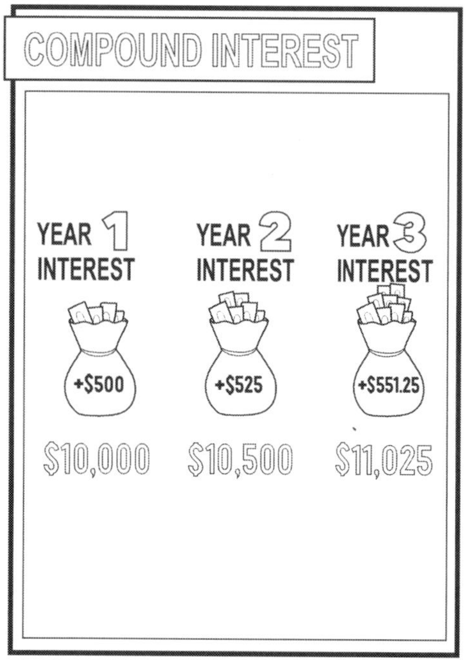

Interest earned on both principal and previously earned interest.

Using the above picture…

How much interest income was generated? ___ + ___ + ___ = _______

Is the interest income unearned income or earned income?

The interest used is 5%. Can you compute what the interest income would be in year five?

Answer: $1,576.25. Unearned. $607.75.

DIVERSIFICATION

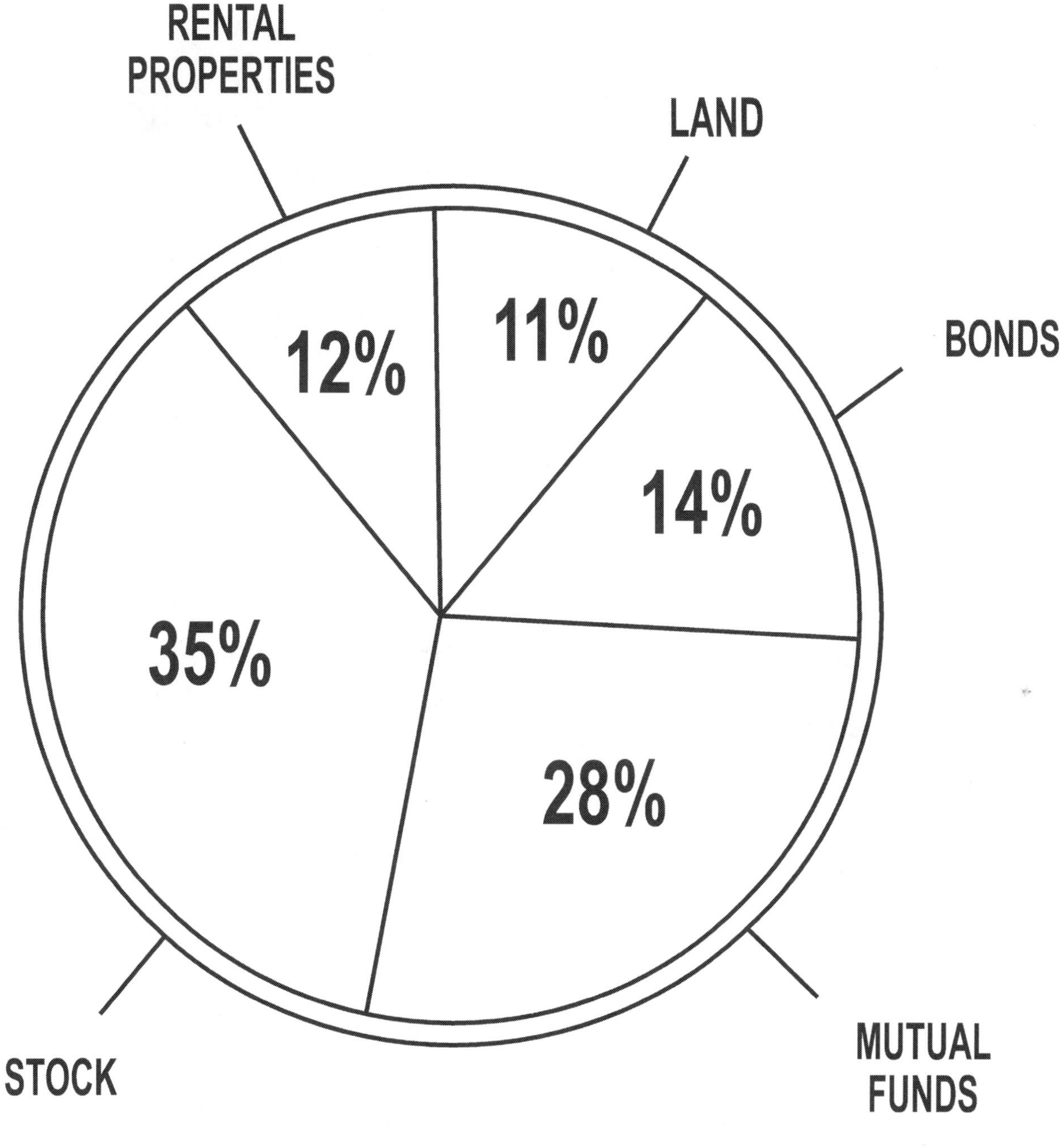

DIVERSIFICATION: A way to reduce risk by spreading your money over a wide variety of investments.

DOLLAR-COST AVERAGING

A method of investing a fixed amount in the same type of investment at regular intervals, regardless of price.

If Marco invest $200 a month how many shares can he buy of ABC stock each month at the below price points?

January- $4:	\$200	÷	\$4	=	______	Shares
February- $2:	______	÷	______	=	______	Shares
March- $5:	______	÷	______	=	______	Shares
April- $10:	______	÷	______	=	______	Shares
May- $20:	______	÷	______	=	______	Shares

Answer: 50, 100, 40, 20, 10.

EQUITY

VALUE: $100,000
MORTGAGE OWED: $50,000

50% EQUITY

EQUITY: Stock ownership in a corporation (shareholder's equity) or the amount of an asset owned (for example if you have a $100,000 home, and you only owe $50,000 on the mortgage, you have 50% equity in the home).

FREE MARKET ECONOMY

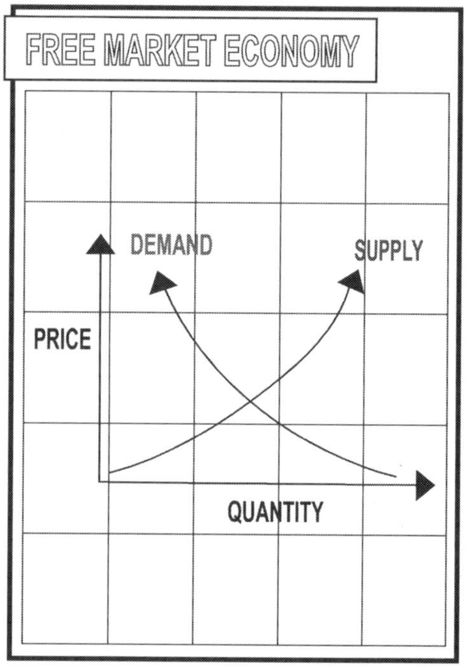

An economy with little or no government involvement and pricing is based on supply and demand.

Use the **grid** to help **draw** the picture!

FUTURE VALUE

FUTURE VALUE

SIMPLE INTEREST

FUTURE VALUE = CURRENT VALUE (1+(INTEREST RATE x NUMBER OF YEARS))

$170 = $100 (1+(.07 x 10))

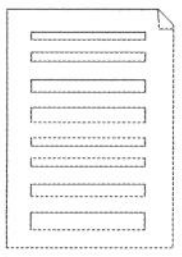

$100

7% (+$7) FOR 10 YEARS

The value of a current asset at a future date based on an assumed rate of growth.

Using the formula determine what the future value is on the following investment.

Current Value = $10,000, Interest Rate = 9%, and Term = 3 Years

Answer: $12,700.

INDEX FUND

A portfolio of stocks or bonds designed to mimic the content and performance of a financial market index.

If you could create your own index fund what ten companies from the S&P 500 would you invest in? Tip-Research what companies are in the S&P 500.

Company Name	Ticker Symbol	Company Name	Ticker Symbol

INFLATION

Decode the Secret Message!

1= A	14= N
2= B	15= O
3= C	16= P
4= D	17= Q
5= E	18= R
6= F	19= S
7= G	20= T
8= H	21= U
9= I	22= V
10= J	23= W
11= K	24= X
12= L	25= Y
13= M	26= Z

23 8 5 14   1   3 21 18 18 5 14 3 25 19

16 21 18 3 8 1 19 9 14 7   16 15 23 5 18   6 1 12 12 19

15 22 5 18   20 9 13 5   12 5 1 4 9 14 7   20 15

8 9 7 8 5 18   16 18 9 3 5 19

Answer: When a currency's purchasing power falls over time, leading to higher prices.

LIQUIDITY

LIQUIDITY

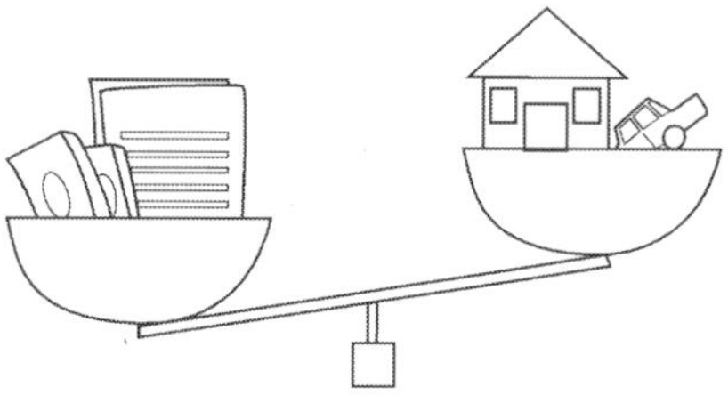

The ease with which an asset or security can be converted into ready cash without affecting its market price; for example, a mutual fund is more liquid than real estate.

Match the asset with its correct liquidity state.

Boat Land Your Home Diamonds Gold Stocks Rare Coins Bonds	Low Liquidity vs. High Liquidity	Car Money Order Rental Property Check Artwork Rare Sports Card Mutual Funds Overstock from Clothing Store

MONOPOLY

MONOPOLY: When a company has almost total control in a sector or industry, giving it an unfair advantage over the competition.

OPPORTUNITY COST

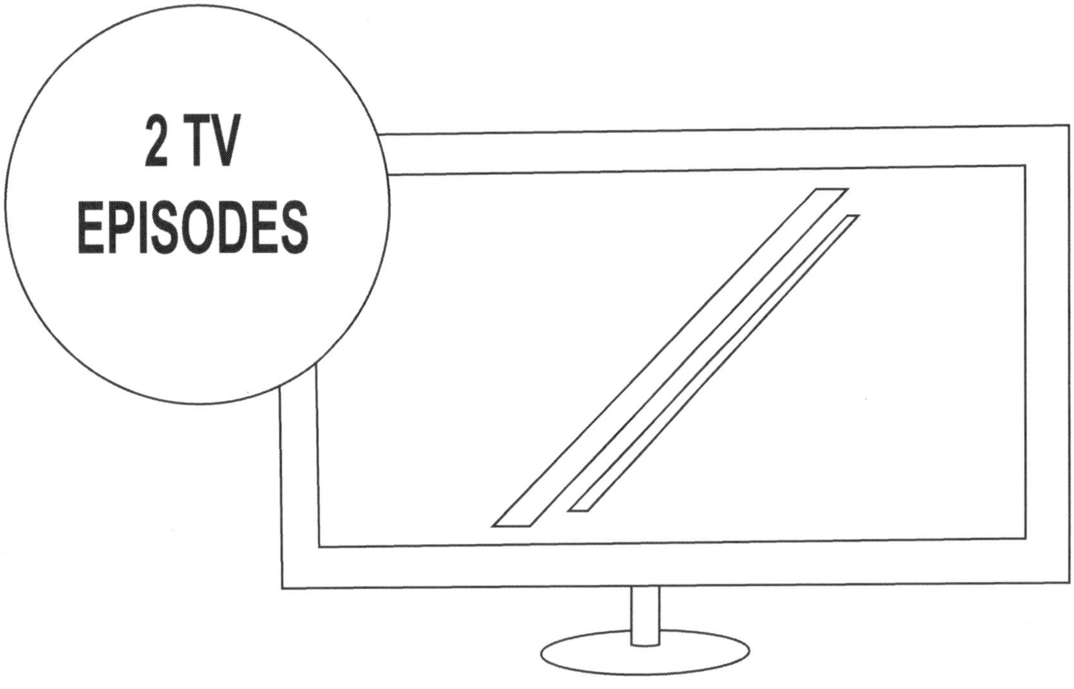

OPPORTUNITY COST: The value of other options that a person gives up when making one choice instead of another; a trade-off.

PRINCIPAL

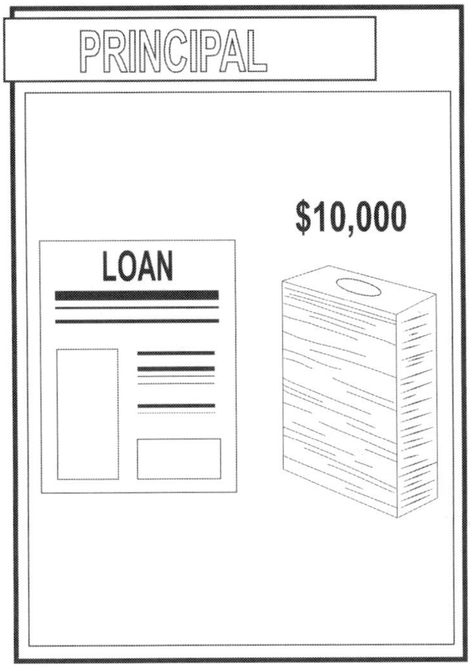

The original amount of money borrowed in a loan or put into an investment.

Match the correct principal with the interest amount.

Total Paid	Total Interest & Fees	Principal
$5,000	$1,500	*$3,500*
$10,000	$2,500	
$50,000	$19,000	
$13,500	$2,900	
$17,400	$2,700	
$500	$80	
$1,000	$225	
$380,000	$120,000	

$420 $7,500 $31,000 $10,600
$14,700 ~~$3,500~~ $775 $260,000

Answer: $3,500, $7,500, $3,100, $10,600, $14,700, $420, $775, $260,000.

RETURN ON INVESTMENT

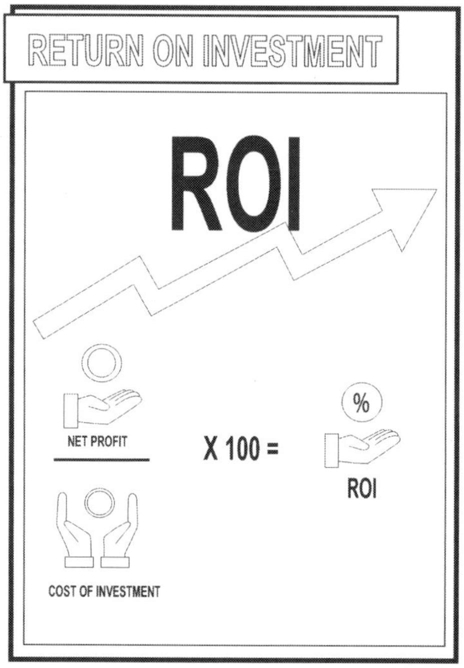

Measures the amount of money earned on an investment compared to the investment's cost.

Catheryn paid $12,000 for an empty lot that she turned into a self-park and pay lot. She paid another $5,500 to develop an app so that payments can be submitted electronically. She also had another $3,000 in cost for things like signs and improvements to the lot. She also pays $1,000 annually to have the parking lot serviced. Her insurance cost for the lot is $1,500 annually. Annual cleaning cost is $6,500.

The lot is just a ten minute walk from the university's football field and a five minute walk from the arena where the basketball teams play. The parking demand is high and Catheryn generates great revenue from her investment. The following are her total sales for the last five years: $25,000, $30,000, $35,000, $43,000, and $28,000.

1. Cost of Investment: (Lot + App)

2. Total 5 Year Expenses

3. Total 5 Year Revenue

5. Total 5 Year ROI

4. Total 5 Year Profit

Answer: $20,500. $45,000 $161,000. $95,500. 466%.

ROTH IRA

1. CONTRIBUTIONS ARE NOT TAX DEDUCTIBLE

2. INVESTMENTS GROW TAX-FREE

ROTH IRA: An account that lets a person save for retirement with contributions (money) that they have already paid taxes on (after-tax); the money may grow tax-free, with tax-free withdrawals in retirement, if certain conditions are met.

RULE OF 72

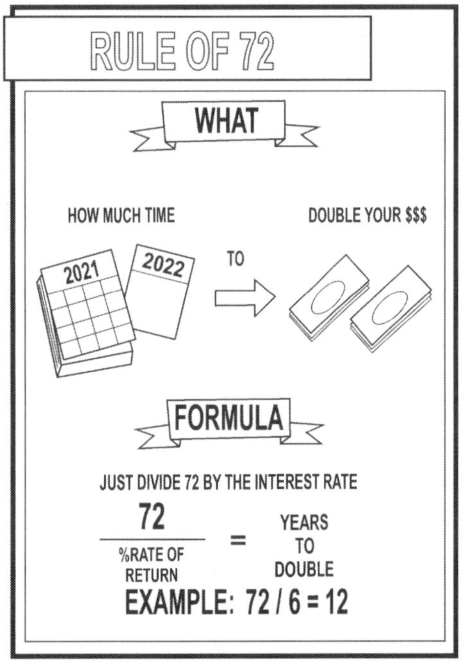

A quick, useful formula that is often used to estimate the number of years it will take to double the invested money at a certain annual rate of return.

Match the correct rate of return with the corresponding time to determine the time frame for doubling the investment. Round to the nearest whole number.

- Rate of Return: 2%
- Rate of Return: 24%
- Rate of Return: 5%
- Rate of Return: 19%
- Rate of Return: 7%
- Rate of Return: 15%
- Rate of Return: 10%
- Rate of Return: 12%
- Rate of Return: 9%

Length of Time in Years

- 14
- 4
- 5
- 36
- 3
- 7
- 6
- 8
- 10

Answer: 36, 3, 14, 4, 10, 5, 7, 6, 8.

TAX CREDIT

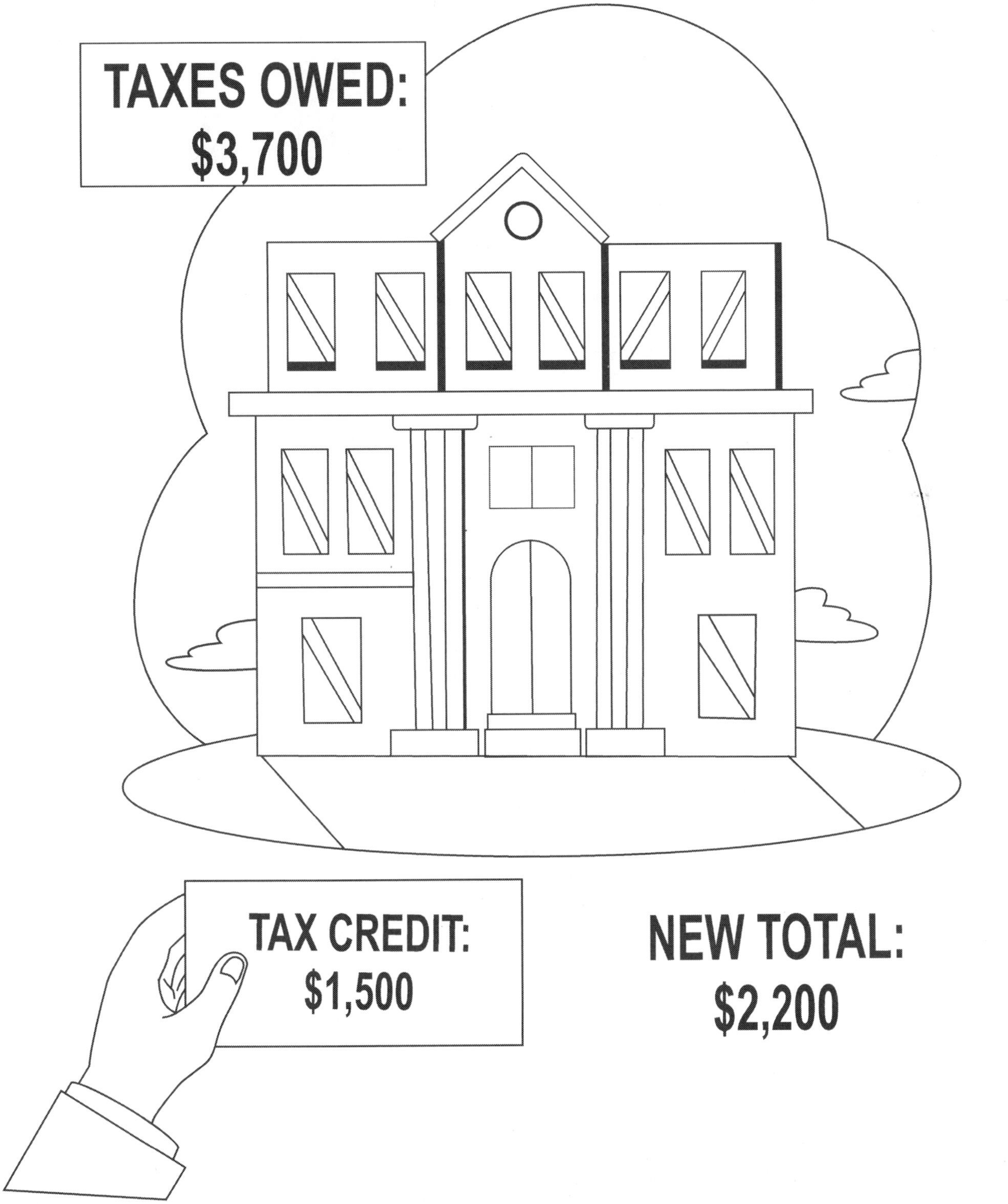

TAX CREDIT: An amount of money that taxpayers can subtract directly from taxes owed to their government; unlike deductions, which reduce the amount of taxable income, tax credits reduce the actual amount of tax owed.

TAX DEDUCTION

EXPENSES:

INSURANCE: $600
REPAIRS: $1,400
ADVERTISING: $600
SUPPLIES: $400
PROPERTY TAXES: $600

TOTAL EXPENSES: $3,600

NET INCOME: $8,400 ← PAY TAXES ON

TAX DEDUCTION: A deduction that lowers a person or organization's tax debt by lowering their taxable income.

TAX DEFERRAL

TAX DEFERRAL: A feature of an investment that postpones taxes due on principal and/or earnings until funds are withdrawn, often at retirement.

TAX EXEMPTION

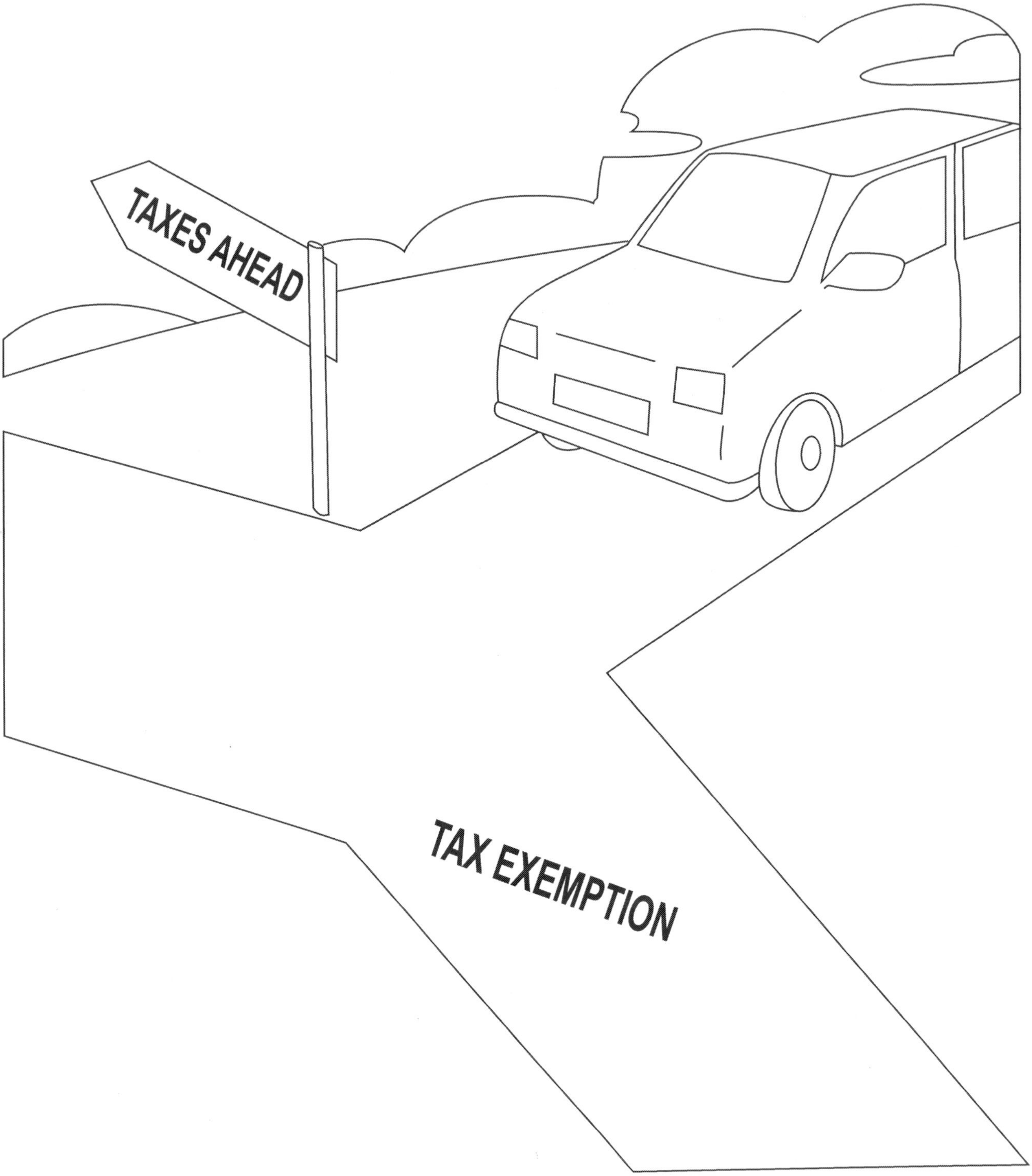

TAX EXEMPTION: Earnings, such as interest from municipal bonds, that are free of certain taxes.

TIME VALUE OF MONEY

Decode the Secret Message!

1= A
2= B
3= C
4= D
5= E
6= F
7= G
8= H
9= I
10= J
11= K
12= L
13= M

14= N
15= O
16= P
17= Q
18= R
19= S
20= T
21= U
22= V
23= W
24= X
25= Y
26= Z

20 8 5   13 15 14 5 25   25 15 21   8 1 22 5

14 15 23   9 19   23 15 18 20 8   13 15 18 5

20 8 1 14   20 8 5   9 4 5 14 20 9 3 1 12

19 21 13   9 14   20 8 5   6 21 20 21 18 5

4 21 5   20 15   9 20 19   16 15 20 5 14 20 9 1 12

5 1 18 14 9 14 7   3 1 16 1 3 9 20 25

Answer: The money you have now is worth more than the identical sum in the future due to its potential earning capacity.

TRADITIONAL IRA

1. FUNDS NOT TAXED UNTIL WITHDRAWN

2. 10% PENALTY ON EARLY WITHDRAWALS

3. BETTER CHOICE IF TAX RATE LOWER AT RETIREMENT

TRADITIONAL IRA: An account that lets a person save for retirement with contributions (money) that they may be able to deduct on their tax return, and any earnings may grow tax-deferred until they withdraw them in retirement.

VOLATILITY

Uncertainty or risk due to the size of changes in a security's value; volatile assets are often riskier than less volatile assets because the price is expected to be less predictable.

Determine if the below description describes a scenario of high volatility (HV) or low volatility (LV).

________ Based on Xavier's research the housing market in his area has continuously increased over the last thirty years.

________ Mya wants to invest in ABC Company. She has discovered that the share price fluctuates widely.

________ Ryan is considering loaning his friend money to start his first business for a 6% return on annual profit.

________ There is a stock that is in a volatile sector. Jessica did her homework and noticed that the stock tends to remain steady during volatile times.

________ Certificates of Deposit (CD's) offer low growth but a guaranteed rate of return.

Answer: LV, HV, HV, LV, LV.

GLOSSARY

1. **APPRECIATION:** When something increases in value.

2. **ASSET:** An item with economic value that a person or organization owns, such as stocks, real estate, personal property, and business equipment.

3. **BANK:** A financial institution that is licensed to receive deposits, offer loans, and provide other financial services.

4. **BANKRUPT:** Describes a person or organization who has been declared by law as unable to pay the debts they owe.

5. **BOND:** A certificate showing that a buyer agrees to lend a business or government money, on the promise that the borrower will pay back the debt—with interest—at a specific time.

6. **BUDGET:** A spending plan or a record of expected and actual income and expenses over a period.

7. **BUSINESS OWNER:** A person or group that owns and profits from a system (business) and its assets without having to be present.

8. **CAPITAL:** Money available to invest.

9. **CHECKING ACCOUNT:** An account that typically holds the money you're using for bill payments and living expenses, usually paying little to no interest.

10. **COLLECTION AGENCY:** A business that specializes in obtaining payments from debtors who have defaulted on their loans.

11. **COMPARISON SHOPPING:** The process of seeking information about products and services to find the best quality or use at the best price.

12. **CONTENTMENT:** Being happy with what you have.

13. **CREDIT**: An agreement to provide goods, services, or money in exchange for future payments with interest by a specific date or according to a specific schedule; the use of someone else's money for a fee.

14. **DEBT**: An amount of money owed to a person, bank, company, etc.

15. **DEPRECIATION:** When something decreases in value.

16. **EARNED INCOME:** Earnings from a job, including commissions and tips.

17. **ECONOMY:** The wealth and resources of a country or region, especially from the goods and services it produces and consumes.

18. **EMERGENCY FUND:** Money set aside for unexpected expenses or for living costs in case of job loss.

19. **EMPLOYEE:** Someone who works for someone else in exchange for wages or a salary.

20. **EXPENSE:** The cost required for something; the money spent on something.

21. **FINANCIAL ADVISER:** A person who provides financial information and advice.

22. **GOODS:** Items that are usually (but not always) tangible, such as pens, salt, apples, and hats.

23. **IMPULSE BUYING:** The buying of goods or services without planning ahead, as a result of a sudden whim or impulse; the buyer often does not consider their needs, goals, or consequences.

24. **INCOME:** Money received, especially on a regular basis, for work or through investments.

25. **INVESTMENT:** The action or process of contributing money to earn a profit or material result.

26. **INVESTOR:** A person or organization that puts money into financial plans, property, etc., expecting to earn a profit.

27. **LIABILITY:** A debt or financial obligation.

28. LOAN: A thing that is borrowed, especially an amount of money that is expected to be paid back with interest.

29. LOSS: An amount of money lost by a business or organization.

30. NEEDS: Things you need to survive.

31. PAY YOURSELF FIRST: The practice of setting aside a portion of all the money you receive for saving and investing before paying other expenses.

32. PROFIT: The money earned after subtracting total costs from the total revenue of a business or investment.

33. RENT: A regular fee for the use of property.

34. REVENUE: Income received from the sale of a product or service.

35. RISK: A measure of chance a loss will happen or an investment will bring a good rate of return.

36. SAVINGS ACCOUNT: A deposit account at a bank or other financial institution that earns interest; it typically pays a modest interest rate, but is safe and reliable, a great way to store cash for short-term needs.

37. SELF-EMPLOYED: Describes someone who works for themselves rather than working for an employer.

38. SERVICE: Work done by other people, such as doctors, lawn care workers, dentists, barbers, and waiters.

39. TICKER SYMBOL: A set of characters—usually letters—representing securities listed on an exchange or otherwise traded publicly.

40. WANTS: Things you do not need to survive.

41. WEALTH: The value of all the assets of worth owned by a person, community, company, or country.

42. 401(k): A company-sponsored retirement account that employees can use to save money. Employers may also contribute the same amount.

43. 52-WEEK HIGH: The highest price at which a security, such as a stock, has traded during a time period equal to one year.

44. 52-WEEK LOW: The lowest price at which a security, such as a stock, has traded during a time period equal to one year.

45. ANNUAL REPORT: A corporate document issued to shareholders that spells out the company's financial condition and operations over the previous year.

46. ANNUITY: A fixed amount of money paid to someone each year, typically for the rest of their life.

47. BENEFICIARY: A person or organization named to receive assets after someone dies.

48. BROKERAGE ACCOUNT: An account to keep cash, liquid money, in for investing in stocks, bonds, mutual funds, and other investments.

49. CAPITAL GAIN: Income from selling an asset for more than the original purchase price.

50. CAPITAL LOSS: A financial loss from selling an asset for less than the original purchase price.

51. COLLATERAL: Property that a borrower promises to give up to a lender in case of default.

52. CONTRACT: A legally binding agreement between two or more parties.

53. CREDIT REPORT: An official record of a borrower's credit history, including such information as the amount and type of credit used, outstanding balances, and any delinquencies, bankruptcies, or tax liens.

54. CREDIT SCORE: A measure of how likely a person applying for a loan is to pay the debt back, based on previous debt repayment.

55. DAY HIGH: The highest price at which a security, such as a stock, has traded that day.

56. DAY LOW: The lowest price at which a security, such as a stock, has traded that day.

57. DEFAULT: Failure to pay a debt or keep a financial agreement.

58. DISPOSABLE INCOME: The amount of money a household has available for spending and saving after paying income taxes.

59. DIVIDENDS: Payments made by publicly listed companies to reward investors for putting their money into the venture.

60. ESTATE: All the money and property owned by a particular person, especially at death.

61. FINANCE CHARGE: A fee charged for the use of credit, which may be a flat fee or a percentage of the amount borrowed; for example, a $100 loan repaid with $9 interest plus a $1 service fee has a finance charge of $10.

62. FINANCIAL PLAN: A document containing a person's current money situation and long-term monetary goals, as well as ways to achieve those goals.

63. FORECLOSURE: A process in which homeowners lose their property because they have failed to make mortgage payments and it becomes the property of the bank.

64. FORTUNE 500: An annual list of the 500 most profitable US industrial corporations.

65. GARNISHMENT: When a court sets aside part of an employee's wages to pay a debt.

66. GRACE PERIOD: A time given for a borrower to pay the full balance of credit due and not incur finance charges or pay an insurance premium without penalty.

67. GROSS PAY: The amount of salary or wages earned by an employee before any deductions or contributions are subtracted, such as taxes.

68. INHERITANCE: Money or property that is passed from one person to another upon the owner's death.

69. INSURANCE: A risk management tool that protects a person from specific financial losses under specific terms and premium payments, as described in a written policy document.

70. INTEREST: The cost of borrowing money and/or the earnings from lending money, which works against you with debt, and for you with investing.

71. NTEREST INCOME: The earnings from lending money.

72. INTEREST RATE: The amount of a loan that the borrower must pay as interest, typically expressed as an annual percentage.

73. LEASE: A contract by which one party lets another use land, property, services, etc. for a specific time, usually in return for a regular payment

74. LEVERAGE: An investment strategy of using debt to try to make more money on an investment.

75. MORTGAGE: A legal agreement by which a bank or other creditor lends money at interest; the lender will own the debtor's property if the debtor defaults on the loan, but not if the debt is paid.

76. MUTUAL FUND: A type of investment vehicle made up of a portfolio of stocks, bonds, or other securities.

77. NET WORTH: A measure of a person's financial condition at a given time, equal to what that person owns (assets) minus what that person owes (liabilities).

78. PORTFOLIO: A collection of securities—such as stocks, bonds, mutual funds, and real estate—that an investor owns.

79. RISK MANAGEMENT: The process of calculating risk and finding ways to lower or manage loss, for example, by buying insurance or diversifying investments.

80. STOCK: An investment that lets the investor own a part of a corporation's assets and earnings.

81. STOCK MARKET: The collection of markets and exchanges where regular buying, selling, and issuance of stock shares of publicly held companies take place.

82. TAX: A government fee on business and personal income, activities, or products.

83. UNEARNED INCOME: Earnings from sources other than a job, including investment returns and royalties.

84. WILL: A legal statement of a person's wishes for giving away his or her estate after death.

85. BEAR MARKET: A time when a market's prices fall for an extended time, usually by 20% or more from recent highs, with negative feelings and low expectations from investors.

86. BULL MARKET: A time when a financial market's prices are rising or are expected to rise.

87. COMPOUND INTEREST: Interest earned on both principal and previously earned interest.

88. DIVERSIFICATION: A way to reduce risk by spreading your money over a wide variety of investments.

89. DOLLAR-COST AVERAGING: A method of investing a fixed amount in the same type of investment at regular intervals, regardless of price.

90. EQUITY: Stock ownership in a corporation (shareholder's equity) or the amount of an asset owned (for example, if you have a $100,000 home, and you only owe $50,000 on the mortgage, you have 50% equity in the home).

91. FREE-MARKET ECONOMY: An economy with little or no government involvement and pricing is based on supply and demand.

92. FUTURE VALUE: The value of a current asset at a future date based on an assumed rate of growth.

93. INDEX FUND: A portfolio of stocks or bonds designed to mimic the content and performance of a financial market index.

94. INFLATION: When a currency's purchasing power falls over time, leading to higher prices for goods and services.

95. LIQUIDITY: The ease with which an asset or security can be converted into ready cash without affecting its market price; for example, a mutual fund is more liquid than real estate.

96. MONOPOLY: When a company has almost total control in a sector or industry, giving it an unfair advantage over the competition.

97. OPPORTUNITY COST: The value of other options that a person gives up when making one choice instead of another; a trade-off.

98. PRINCIPAL: The original amount of money borrowed in a loan or put into an investment.

99. RETURN ON INVESTMENT: Measures the amount of money earned on an investment compared to the investment's cost

100. ROTH IRA: An account that lets a person save for retirement with contributions (money) that they have already paid taxes on (after-tax); the money may grow tax-free, with tax-free withdrawals in retirement, if certain conditions are met.

101. RULE OF 72: A quick, useful formula that is often used to estimate the number of years it will take to double the invested money at a certain annual rate of return.

102. TAX CREDIT: An amount of money that taxpayers can subtract directly from taxes owed to their government; unlike deductions, which reduce the amount of taxable income, tax credits reduce the actual amount of tax owed.

103. TAX DEDUCTION: A deduction that lowers a person or organization's tax debt by lowering their taxable income.

104. TAX DEFERRAL: A feature of an investment that postpones taxes due on principal and/or earnings until funds are withdrawn, often at retirement.

105. TAX EXEMPTION: Earnings, such as interest from municipal bonds, that are free of certain taxes.

106. TIME VALUE OF MONEY: The potential of an investment to gain value by earning interest.

107. TRADITIONAL IRA: An account that lets a person save for retirement with contributions (money) that they may be able to deduct on their tax return, and any earnings may grow tax-deferred until they withdraw them in retirement.

108. VOLATILITY: Uncertainty or risk due to the size of changes in a security's value; volatile assets are often riskier than less volatile assets because the price is expected to be less predictable.

Made in United States
Troutdale, OR
11/03/2026

56847407R00064